Bipolar DX

Bipolar DX

My Inner Dragons

Patricia M. Sherman

To order additional copies of this book, contact:
Xlibris Corporation
1-888-795-4274
www.Xlibris.com
Orders@Xlibris.com
80351

Dedicated to

My Doctor Who Saved Me

My Co-Workers Who Put Up With Me

My Family Who Supported Me

And God Who Made It All Possible

I reach into the medicine cabinet and take out the almost full bottle of aspirin. I pull down the glass by the tooth brushes and fill it with water. Taking several aspirin in my hand I begin the process of swallowing the entire bottle. I know that this will make me very sick or kill me, which is my intention.

I feel very sad and I want to get away from it all. My parents are downstairs having an argument. Over what, I have no idea. All I know is it is Christmas Eve and I remember that this fight happens every year when everything just starts falling apart and the arguing begins. It just figured to me that if I were to die the arguing would stop and Christmas would be much happier. This is my first suicidal gesture.

At some point I begin to think a little more rationally and realize that I have little or no conception of what is going to happen to me when I die. And I become alarmed and want the process to end. Being in the Girl Scouts and having won my first aid badge, I remembered that warm salty water will make me throw up and if I throw up the aspirin I will be out of danger and will not die at all.

I sneak down the stairs and into the kitchen and get a glass of warm, almost hot water. I find the large box of cooking salt and put so much into the water that it does not even dissolve all the way. I creep back upstairs to the bathroom and with trepidation swallow the entire glassful of the noxious fluid. It does not take long to work. I begin to throw up into the toilet for what seems like forever. When I am done I am spent and crawl to my room falling onto my bed to sleep, if able, or to hide if necessary. I wake up the next day sick as a dog with an incessant ringing in my ears. The atmosphere in the house has lightened up and my parents thought I had the flu. I do not ever tell anyone what I have done. I am 10 years old.

Going to the party was the last thing that I wanted to do, but my mother said that I was to go, so go I did. I was not a popular kid in school and was usually asked to these parties because they were class parties and the parents would invite the entire class. I could not get into the games and activities as I was clumsy and very shy. I would end up sitting in the corner of the room watching and praying that the time would go by swiftly so my mother could come and pick me up soon. I had at times simply gone out onto the porch for most of the party to wait. No one ever noticed that I was gone. This is a behavior that stayed with me well into adulthood and still today creeps back into my way of handling gatherings of people, including my own family.

I was very much a tom-boy. I would rough house with the boys, play baseball, football, war (it was the fifties and war was appropriate for the times). The only thing I could not do was climb trees. When I was starting to develop—which was early in the sixth grade—the boys wanted to see what my chest looked like so I lifted up my shirt and showed them. They wanted to kiss me and I let them. They wanted to see the difference in boy vs. girl anatomy so I showed them and let them touch. I was not respected, but was "one-of-the-boys", so I allowed sexual overtones. I even watched jerk-off circles. I was hideously jealous of the boy's equipment and wanted at that time to change into a boy.

I had an incestuous relationship with my brother short of penetration. This was all my idea. This may have gone on for much longer than it did, but I shot my mouth off to the boy down the street and he told his mother, who in turn told mine, who in turn had a chat with my brother and I. Now I was masturbating every chance I had.

Sleep overs were always interesting with the girl down the street. I have no idea who initiated it, but we had a homosexual relationship with the two of us kissing and rubbing against each other. I was very good at this and could get positioned over the pubic bone and bring myself to orgasm. I was also able to do this with the boy across the street and the knoll post of my bed. I could not get enough. I was 11.

Oh! Holy Menarche. The day you become a woman. I went to the bathroom one day and when I wiped myself there was this dark brown substance all over the toilet paper. I was frightened out of my mind. I didn't know what it was and thought that I was dying. I called out for my mother and she came and looked, then disappeared into the bathroom closet and came out with a pad and belt and said, "Put this on and you will be OK." Put this on? How? Where? OK from what? How do you know? WHAT IS ALL THIS? My first period and that is the information I was given. I am 12 ½.

I woke up one morning in a world of hurt, especially around the knees. I could hardly move them. I felt very weary and tried to sleep on the couch most of the day, but my mother did not like this and told me that I was malingering and to get up and do my chores around the house. She thought that I had merely "stressed" my knees playing chicken at the local swimming pool the day before. By Monday it was apparent that I was in deep trouble as I was unable to get out of bed. The pain was like tiny lances racing in and out of my knees and then spreading up along my back.

The doctor was summoned and came to the house. Then from the house I was taken to the hospital and was diagnosed with Rheumatic Fever. I was about to start a medically imposed prison sentence of six weeks. I was allowed to get up out of bed only to go to the bathroom. My father used to pick me up and take me to his bedroom in the morning so I could watch television some days. I was bought an orthopedic mattress and a radio to fill out my days and nights as I could not sleep for the pain. My mother washed my legs down with alcohol and wintergreen then wrapped them in hot towels for the pain. Then came the great and wonderful day when I was allowed to come down onto the porch to sit for several hours in the spring air. I was allowed to come down one stair at a time on my rear end then up the same way. I could do this once a day. In the mean time I missed the last day of eighth grade, the class party, and the class pool party. As July turned to August, I was cleared to go on vacation with my family.

During this vacation that took us from Cumberland, Maryland to California, my father was called by his company and notified that he was being transferred to Salt Lake City, Utah. We were two families traveling together at the time. Me with my parents and my brother, my aunt and uncle and their daughter. My brother finished the tour with my aunt and uncle and due to my recent illness, I went back home with my parents to pack. I always felt that my brother got the better part of the bargain. The next several years, being the ever moody child, things were very quiet, until I was on the lawn wrestling with my brother and another boy that we had known back east. My mother took me into the house and explained that I could not go on doing this "sort of thing" as I was now 14. It was not "proper". Proper was never defined and I was left confused. I was later presented with an article from a '50's magazine called Blue Jeans and Petticoats, by "Dear Abby". Laughable by today's standards, this was in way of explaining what proper and improper was for the late '50's early '60's. It never did explain what "Don't let a boy touch you" meant, and I heard that a lot, and this was whether I was dating or not, mostly not. I was still awkward and shy, sitting in corners.

I went to three schools in Salt Lake City. One middle school and two high schools. I was never a problem to the teachers and apparently never really was anything special in class or with my classmates. I would guess that this was a period of normalcy. I did not excel much in regular classes, but was good in drama, art and science. I simply did not stand out as anyone who was anyone you would want to be with or know. There were no real dates and no fast friends. I was very much the loner. I did have one friend that walked to school with me every morning, but I think that was only because I passed by her house going to one school and she passed mine going to another. I was asked out once. I got dressed up and eagerly awaited my date. In the meantime my parents went out. The boy never came and I went to bed weeping knowing he was with his friends laughing at me. I never told my parents so they were none the wiser.

In my early teen aged years my mother started to get on my "case" about being too heavy. She would harangue me about what I was eating and how much exercise I was or was not doing, the size of my clothes. She threatened not to buy me any more clothes or not to make any more clothes after a certain size. She got me up early to watch the "Jack LaLane Show", monitored my meals, even took me to a "fat" doctor. He did some blood tests and put me on thyroid medicine. Told me that fat girls turn into fat women. The medicine made me edgy and unable to sleep. I was very quick to snap at people. Oh, I lost 10 pounds, but at what cost?

During all this, my mother had surgery for breast cancer. I had an appendectomy and my brother had a gynecomastectomy (removal of enlarged breast glands). After all of this, I became very "moody". I did not like coming out of my room and I did not want to go out of the house. I didn't much like being with my family. My mother made me angry one day and I wrote in my diary that I wished that she would just up and die somewhere and leave us all alone already. Thinking rather foolishly that this would remain between me and the diary. I was very very wrong.

Mom read my diary and to this day I wonder if she had been reading it all along. What a terrible thought. All of my "I would never say these things to anyone ever" thoughts were in there. She was, of course, only months away from the mastectomy that she had to endure for the cancer that they found in her right breast. She went into a fury at first which totally crushed my father. He in turn came to me and with the harshest of words and tone told me how horrid a daughter I was and he wished he had never set eyes on me. After the fury came tears and depression. I in turn became very depressed, but this was seen as a ploy for attention. I stayed in my room, slept long hours, went nowhere out of the house with the exception of school and church. I cried a lot. Long hours were spent asking God to forgive me for such an unforgivable wish. One just does not wish their parents dead. Especially when the one you're wishing about has a terminal illness.

Graduating from high school was major for me. I wanted in the worst way to go to the prom graduation night. Can you believe what a gross turn off it would be not to go? Everyone in the class, whether they ever saw you again or not, would know you were not worthy enough to be asked . . . by anyone.

I decided I was going and fixed my sights on a fellow who was known as an egg head. I guess nerd is the word today. Purely fastidious, academic, and dull. One night during an MYF (Methodist Youth Fellowship) meeting, we ended up on the lawn, gazing—if you could call it that—at the stars. I started up about the prom and how important it was to a youth's development—trying the intellectual approach—to go to the prom. How important it was to learning socialization and maturation. I laid it on thicker than WD40. He had counter arguments about the frivolity of the whole thing and besides who would want to go with him? Man, I jumped on that. The fellow was not bad looking. He was just . . . how can I say it? A stick in the mud. He was, however, my only chance for the prom and I worked every angle until he relented and I had my date for the prom.

We went and I acted a pure fool. Hyper and laughing and dancing around even without partner or music. I practically left him at the door and maneuvered through the gym to speak with all the folks I felt to be important. Can you imagine not wanting to go in the first place then being "dumped" at the door? Pathetic. I should have been shot! Well, it mattered not to me as I was leaving for the East Coast in the morning with my mother and brother. I would never see this boy again.

My mother had always kept great distance between us. It was like when we were in the same room she made sure I was at least an arm's length away. I do not remember many hugs or kisses. No "That's my girl". No "I love you." She even had a game we would play. I would say "You're my Mommy" and she would reply "No, doorstep baby". In this game she would never relent and say yes you are my baby after all. But she did many things for me that other mothers did not do for their children. She taught me how to sew and cook. She made things for me like most of my clothes when I was growing up. She had more energy than any person I knew. She canned in the fall, painted, wallpapered, took classes at the high school, did wood working. I can remember when she sanded and refinished all the floors in the house. It was go, go, go.

My mother did encourage me to do some things in life and did express some satisfaction that I was able to do them well. Always at a distance, I was encouraged to apply myself in the fine arts, painting and calligraphy. Acting was something that she thought I did rather well. She felt that I was talented in the sciences and she insisted that nursing was an "honorable" profession and encouraged me to go in that direction for my life's work. Actually I had expressed a love of animals and early in life remarked to my parents that I would like to be a veterinarian. My mother had a fit and said, "No daughter of mine is going to be up to here—shoulder—in some filthy old cow." So that went by the way real quick.

The day after graduation from high school, we packed up and moved back to Cumberland, Maryland, a quaint little town known as the Queen City as it sat nestled in a valley surrounded by mountains in the Appalachian range. This was a re-visitation as this is where my story began. I was now in nurse's training and my brother was finishing his senior year in high school. My father was working for Hercules Powder Company and my mother was "running" the household. She continues to show an enormous amount of energy until the second year we were there. She began to have vague aches and pains in her hip joints. This turned out to be metastasized cancer from her breast CA. Over the next two years she would have cobalt therapy, hormonal therapy, and her pituitary gland removed in the hopes of arresting the disease.

As I was the "nurse in the family," it fell upon me to explain things and help my mother with daily care. I was totally inadequate to the task as I was still only a student. I did not know what was going on or what I was expected to do. Consequently, I would make mistakes and my mother would flare up into a rage or would fall to pieces in tears. Her mood was extremely labile and I put it down to the fact that she was dying. During all of this my mother remained steadfast in her support of my becoming a registered nurse.

After the first year of training we were "capped", a ceremony where the freshman students are presented with the caps they were to wear for the next two years. Mother, who was deathly ill due to the cobalt, was in the back of the room with baggies in her hand so if she should become sick she could throw up into the baggie and not make a mess while she got herself to the bathroom. She was, however, there to "see her little girl get capped". That was also the day that I gave my first injection to a live person—my mother. During the cobalt the doctor started my mother on a regimen of Drolban, a male hormone similar to testosterone. Hopefully, as they had just destroyed her ovaries with cobalt, the testosterone would wipe out all vestiges of the female hormones and arrest the cancer. My father was unable to give the injections so it came to me to do the dirty work.

After the capping we went to my room with an instructor. It took me several attempts, but I finally was able to get the needle in. I pressed the plunger and to my horror realized I had not aspirated—pulled back on the plunger to make sure the needle was not in a vein. Next time she came to get her shot she bent over, pulled down her pants and scrawled across her backside was the word ASPIRATE written in mercurochrome—my father had done this. Well! I never forgot again.

This turned out to be a devastating treatment. My mother would come to the school once or twice a week and I would give her the shots. The medication ravaged my mother's body. She grew hair on her face, she had fatty redistribution, her voice lowered and she lost her rear end. The fatty distribution was awful as it made her look as though she were made of clay and someone had scooped out some and left a hole and put some back and made a lump—all over her body. My mother had been a real beauty. She looked so much like Ingrid Bergman that in her youth people would come up to her and ask for an autograph. Now she resembled a pathetic old man and I was responsible for this. Me alone. I am the one that gave her those injections. I'm the one who pumped that noxious hormone into my mother's body and the result was horrific. All my fault that she was now so unattractive. All my fault.

That year in July, I think, I was to have a month off before starting my senior year with my psychiatric training at Springfield State Hospital. My mother was deteriorating a little and my father wanted me to take care of her while I was off and then defer my psych training to take care of her for as long as she had left. This was not to be. Being as labile as she was, there finally came a day when she became hysterical and screamed at my father about how horrid I had been to her all day and that she wanted me out of the house. My father never did tell me exactly what it was that had my mother so upset that day. She had been very sick all day long and I had changed her and the bed and washed her and the linens and given her medicine and patted her. I had no idea what I could possibly have done to have upset her so. I was, however, shown the door when my psych rotation came around. I actually went with relief. At that point I was exhausted.

Psychiatric training for our school was at Springfield State Hospital in Sykesville, Maryland, some 135 miles away from home. As my parents were not very thrilled with me I had decided to remain there until it was time to go back to school. This meant that I would be there over the weekends, most likely alone as most students bolted to their cars and beat a hasty retreat back to Cumberland every Friday afternoon. I was not fated to be alone; however, as I was going to meet the man of my dreams.

There were three schools of nursing students represented at the Jones Building (our residence), and I found a friend from Lutheran Hospital by the name of Carroll who in turn became friendly with a fellow that worked at Springfield by the name of Bunky. Bunky had a friend named Byron and I had seen the two of them around. I was of the opinion that Byron was a simpleton, buffoon, a jester. He was just too silly for words with his jumping around, playing games and joking with everyone. I really did not like him much. That was to change.

One night while sitting on the Jones Building steps I hear, "There she is. My favorite Patti Sherman." I looked up, but was unable to see because of the ground level lights on the walkway. Next thing I knew I was thrown back onto the steps and righteously kissed on the mouth. I was let loose breathless and stunned. I righted myself to find that I was sitting next to Byron Paul Greene, PA (psychiatric aide) extraordinaire, his arm draped over my shoulder. I was not only speechless but furious and strangely excited. Over the course of about an hour we spoke of many things when suddenly Byron asked if I liked to go to carnivals. I said yes and he jumped up and said he'd pick me up the next night and take me to one. At that point as much as I anticipated the best, I was definitely expecting the worst. That I had just been set up to be stood up. Just like in high school.

Even though I expected to be stood up I was ready and waiting on the steps of the residence, when lo and behold down the street from the men's residence came Mr. Greene in his tiny cream Opal Cadet with a bat silhouette on the sides. The Bat Mobile had arrived. A three shift that could hardly do 50 miles an hour in a fierce tail wind. This was to be our chariot from now on. In I got and away we went to an unknown future. This being our first date we talked about everything, what we liked and did not like, music, movies, cars, travel, and children. We had known each other for 24 hours and this man is asking me about children—when, where, and how many. Our first date for crying out loud and we were quietly discussing children. From that moment we were inseparable, having breakfast every morning and dinner in the evening and going out every night until 1 am and all day Saturday and Sunday.

One day Byron asked me about a trip to the shore. We were to go to the shore for an overnight trip. Being a virgin and very naïve I was to call the shots. As Byron had already let me know that he slept in his shorts I told him that he would have to find a full pair of pajamas to sleep in with me, this meant full top and bottoms. I would wear a long granny gown. There was to be no sex. I was so excited I quivered as I prayed the rules would be honored and somewhere inside hoped that they wouldn't as this was the man for me—my "Mr. Right, my Mr. Wonderful, my Knight in Shining Armor." Well, you get the idea. He told me he would have to borrow something as he had no PJ's with him. The rules were set and he went forth to find suitable night wear.

We went to Ocean City, Maryland, to the Ebb Tide Motel. A tiny hole in the wall about five or six miles away from the shoreline. By got out of the car to get the room and I sat in the car and tried to look the dutiful wife waiting for her man. The room was an efficiency with a sink, fridge, stove and all the equipment needed to cook. It was small and cozy and clean. By went to take a shower and when he came out I went into gales of laughter. I could not help it as the PJ's he had got were too small and looked as though they were for a 14 year old. They were a bright yellow knit with navy cuffs and were about six inches too short on the legs and the arms. I couldn't help myself. He had gone to such lengths to get these just for me and I stood there laughing at them, however, I knew that if they stayed on I would be out of danger. I wore a long pink and white granny gown gathered under the bust and to the floor with puffed sleeves. Byron found it enchanting. We were perfect together that night. Laughing and kissing, holding on to one another, and cuddling. We put on the brakes when we realized that my top had been pulled down and there was a bit of kissing and holding on to my breasts; so we went to "sleep" spooned up against each other, remaining pristine.

One Saturday afternoon my Aunt Suzy called me at the residence with a warning not to tell my father that she had called. My mother was in the hospital across from the residence in Cumberland. He had specifically told her not to call so as not to interrupt my studies. Aunt Suzy decided to call because it was obvious to her that I needed to come home right away. They were telling my mother that she had pneumonia, but it was obvious to everyone that it was the cancer, metastasized from her bones to her lungs, and this was going to be her last fight. She was dying and there was not a thing to be done but get there as soon as possible without raising suspicion with my father. One of my classmates called her mother and she came and picked us up and drove us all the way to Cumberland just so I could go see my mother. I have always thought that to be extraordinarily kind.

When we got to the residence I called my father at home with the story that at the last moment one of the girls decided to come home and I decided to come with her. He then asked me if I had been to the hospital yet. I played dumb and asked why and he countered with the fact that Aunt Suzy told on herself and he knew I was coming. So much for my play of innocence. So I went to see my mother for the first time in almost three months. This turned out to be one of the hardest things I would ever do.

Standing at the door I saw a pale critically ill woman who was in pain, restless and miserable. I walked and I touched her arm and whispered her name. She awoke with a start, hysterical and fighting, shouting "NO! NO! NOT AGAIN!" She was flailing her arms around in the air as if warding off someone or something and with that I saw a horrible, huge, livid bruise on her arm from below the crook of her elbow to above apparently from blood draws. I was appalled. She was obviously delirious and had no idea who I was. I left the room in tears. The waiting room was right across the hall and my aunt, uncle, grandmother and father and brother were waiting for me.

I was beset by questions as I was "the nurse in the family," something I was going to hear a lot in the next few days. It was understood by all that Mom would not be leaving the hospital alive. The question was when and how her end would come. I was questioned repeatedly about what to look for and what to listen for to know that her dying was imminent. My aunt was the most insistent, haranguing me for information—even though I was still a student and so vey uninformed—yet she felt that I had to have an answer for her and the rest of the family. So I told them the most obvious thing I could think of and that was she would become very cold in her lower extremities. She would be very quiet and probably sleep her way out of this world into the next. My poor aunt took me at my word and would pull up the covers and touch her feet every time she went into the room, then sit with her hands on her feet and wait for them to go cold.

The pressure about all of this was telling. I became most fatigued and found it hard to stay alert. After spending a long while in Mom's room I went out to the waiting room with the whole clan, but could not get a handle on it anymore, so I went to another waiting room to lie down for awhile and fell asleep. When I woke up and went back to our waiting room my father was waiting with scathing anger. If I could not stay awake then what good was I? I might as well go back to school and let everything go on without me. As it happened, my mother had eventually realized who I was and knew that I was supposed to have been 135 miles down the road, so why was I here? I have never been a good liar and was not then. I came up with some cock-and-bull story and that I would be going right back to school. After all, she did not need me as she only had pneumonia. My mother was not a stupid woman and she knew very well that this was the end and that there was no pneumonia. She played the game rather well though, complaining of how people with pneumonia did suffer. Sad as it was, I knew she knew and I knew she knew that I knew and we just left it unsaid. Sad because it prevented me from ever having the chance to say goodbye, but that was the game we were playing. The other game that was played was the you're my mommy game and no doorstep baby. At this point my mother could not talk, but she managed a "nu-hu"—denied me to the last. She just would not give it up.

My father wanted me to go back because he thought I did not care enough. My aunt was furious that I was going because she thought I was going to "be with your boyfriend", making me the most horrid of daughters. So what is the toll so far? My mother understood why I was going back, my father thought me worthless and my aunt believed me to be the most thoughtless of daughters. This was not good for my self esteem or my feelings of well-being especially as I knew that my reasons for leaving were actually pure in heart. So, this dreadful daughter did slowly slink back to school with her tail between her legs and with a filthy black cloud enveloping all her senses.

The phone call came while By and I were out at another carnival with friends. He took me to the residence and as I had some time we stood on the porch and snuggled before I had to go in. The house mother came and suggested that I come in now. I reminded her I still had some time. She insisted and with one last kiss I was off. When I got to my floor all the lights were on and everyone was awake and waiting for me. I knew at that moment that my mother was dead. She died about 10:00 pm that evening about the time we decided to quit the carnival and go get something to eat. I was out on a date when my mother died. I was out having fun with my boyfriend while my mother was dying. I had not been thinking about her at all. Even though I knew that she was going to die soon, I put it out of my mind to have fun with my boyfriend. How callused can a person be? I guess they had all been right after all. I had gone back to my boyfriend and could have cared less. My brother would pick me up in the morning and take me home. I am 19.

It was a nice funeral as funerals go, I guess. I really had nothing to gauge it by as I had never been involved with one. My mom had discussed what she wanted with my father long before it was needed so everything that she wanted was there. She wanted to be transported in the blue station wagon, but as that was not practical due to weight and size a blue hearse was found instead. She did not want flowers, but wanted it to be announced that donations to the Cancer Society would be more appreciated. She ended up getting both. She wanted to be buried in her traveling suit as wherever she was going she would be traveling, also, she wanted her walking shoes as wherever she went she would be on her feet. She asked for a Methodist hymnal as "No one can sing like us Methodists," and she insisted that she have a St. Christopher's medal to get her there safely and a menorah to light her way. The pastor gave the hymnal and a friend gave the medal and I gave the menorah that she had given to me the last Christmas. All this in the light blue coffin which was another of her requests.

The weather was lousy with wind and rain, breaking a two month drought. But coincidentally it only rained while we were indoors and not transferring her from one place to another. It also stopped raining while we were in the cemetery and resumed when we were all back in our cars. Pop said it was Mom's doing. That she had gone to God and told him to get his act together. The flowers were wilting. It was over except for the hard feelings from while she was in the hospital. My aunt would have nothing to do with me and my father said that if I continued to smoke that I could not be my mother's daughter. My brother was too bereft to say anything and my grandma; well, she loved me no matter what. She was the only one in the family that seemed to have a grasp on the situation. I went back to Springfield to finish my psych rotation.

My Lord, was I depressed by this time. Let's face it, I ruined my mother with medication, I did not see her for almost two months, I left her to die without me, and I alienated most of my family. The only support I had at this time was Byron and it was not enough. One gray day, after a considerable amount of rainfall, I found myself sitting in my fourth floor window, sans screen, thinking about jumping to my death. I was all the way out onto the sill when it occurred to me that with the ground as wet as it was I would only bounce and cripple myself for the rest of my life. This was not my intention as pain was not what I was looking for but the release of it. I was on my way back into the room when someone came in and saw me and thought I was on the way out. They came barging into the room pulling me out of the window yelling for help. I got it all right, just not that very instant. I woke up several days later and while I was taking my bath before class I broke out into the most florid case of hives I have yet to see to this day. I was red and bumpy from head to toe and itch? It was agony. I was taken to the infirmary and examined then given antihistamines for the itching. The problem was that they only made me woozy and stupid while the itching continued. It was only then that I was to see a psychiatrist. It was thought that the hives were psychosomatic as a side effect of depression.

I was shown into the doctor's office, which was the admission office to the hospital, and introduced to the doctor. I wish I could remember his name as he was the first to treat me. We spoke with one another and he drew out of me what had been going on and that I was not feeling so well. He understood the problem and prescribed Aventyl (nortriptyline) for the depression—my first drug for a mental disorder. It not only made me feel as though I was outside of my body observing everything from across the room, but gave me a terrible taste in my mouth that Byron said he could taste when he kissed me. When I went home for a visit, I told my father about everything that was going on with the hives and the depression and he hit the ceiling. He did not believe in depression, he did not believe in psychiatrists, he did not think that anyone anywhere at any time should be on "those kinds of drugs." So, no support there.

Support was to be had, however, in Byron. He really loved me and showed his support daily with his ability to listen and his soft spoken wisdom and humor. He was a funny man. I met his family at last and it was then we decided that it would be a good thing to marry. His mother was sort of stand-offish, but his father was just like him, outgoing with a charming sense of humor. I had him eating out of my hand. He had three brothers all younger and a sister who was next to him in age. She and I shared a room together the night I stayed over and we talked and laughed and exchanged notes on her brother all night. The next morning I noticed that Margaret (Mrs. Greene), did not seem to be quite as stiff. Later she would tell me that Carol (By's sister), told her that she really liked me and hoped that Byron would marry me. We had not announced our plans as yet. This was just a getting to know you trip. Later Margaret would tell me that she knew he was going to marry me because he had never brought a girl home to meet the family before he brought me.

My grandfather died just eight months after my mother. He had been in a mental institution for some years with cerebral athrosclerosis and senile dementia—known as Alzheimer's today. At 88 he fell and fractured his hip, got pneumonia and died. His funeral was quiet with a few interesting things thrown into his coffin for luck. He was buried in his "western" suit from Salt Lake City, which he never wore while he was alive, his Stetson hat, that he always wore, a plaid shirt with flora tie and can-can dancer tie clasp. Just as in real life. We also threw in a statue of the Lion of Lucerne, from Switzerland, as that is where he was from. Pop insisted that there was something missing and we all agreed that the scotch he always had with him was just the thing. So Pop went to a drug store to get an "expectorant" bottle to put it in. After purchasing a high grade of scotch and transferring some into the little bottle, it fell upon me to put it into his inside coat pocket. I was after all, "the nurse in the family." That done we retired home to toast the old man, knowing that wherever he was, he was laughing his rear end off at us.

The wedding was set to go off in June. The caterer was engaged and the church set up and the dress and get away dress obtained. Pop wanted to give me a huge wedding with all the trimmings and a dress to match, but I would have none of it. Byron's family was not affluent and as they were coming from so far away, I did not want to spend a lot of money on the wedding. It would be too much like showing off. Pop only agreed if the reception could be his and he could do whatever he liked with it. I agreed. Off we went to our prospective corners to get things done. I lined up the neighbor across the street as my matron of honor and my brother's girl friend as bride's maid. They were to wear whatever they had that was colorful and dressy. Byron had Bunky as his best man and my brother as a groomsman. They were to wear everyday suits.

I gave up my room and bed to my grandmother and did not sleep a wink the night before. Mostly due to the fact that I was relegated to sleep on the couch. Byron lost the toss and had to sleep in the same bed as Bunky and did not sleep a wink the night before. So, to the organ music of "Trumpet Tune" and I don't know what, we went up and down the aisle. My minister and Byron's father read us our vows. Mr. Greene was a Brethren minister and I was insistent that he have something to do with the ceremony. I had his undying affection from that day on. It was a good idea and everyone thought it went very well. With a lot of laughing and kissing and rice throwing we retired to my house where the reception was all set up with wet and dry punches to satisfy all attending. Pop out did himself and it was better than wonderful. With a "High Ho Silver" and an "Up, Up and Away," we were off for an overnight "honeymoon", then back to school. I thought I was deliriously happy. I was now a married woman and about to begin an odyssey of thirteen years that would forever mark my life. I was 20.

Somewhere along the line with me so intent on getting married I failed to realize that my father was also going to tie the knot. He had met a woman from work, a Linda Nolan, and started to take her out. Now, I had met some of the ladies my father had gone out with since my mother had died and they were all mature and had children of their own, grown up and out of the house and I approved of one in particular. I thought she would be wonderful for my father and for me especially. Not a selfish bone in my body, you hear? He, however, had different ideas of what he was looking for and started to date Linda very seriously. So seriously that he was out until all hours on Christmas Eve. Something that had never happened in our family, as that was a night everyone was expected to be home whether there was an argument or not.

When I found out how serious he was about this woman I had a fit. She was only five years older than I was, had a one year old son, was divorced, smoked—and you remember the remark after the funeral about smoking—was totally unsophisticated, and could not sew or cook. What was he thinking? Apparently he was thinking that he was in love with her.

The announcement was made at my wedding reception after I had gone and caused a furor as it had not yet been a whole year since my mother's demise. My aunt, who was now speaking to me disowned him right then and there and was destined to never speak to him again. If this could happen in such a short period then that must mean that he knew her before Mom died and he had tryst with her. The no-good-nick! His friends were aghast as she was a secretary at the plant where he worked, so was for all intents a "nobody" and my father being a "somebody" should never have even given her the time of day. Well, the damage was done and in July they were married to a sparse crowd and without me. I could not bring myself to go watch the unholy union. Instead Byron and I went to the shore for our "real" honeymoon.

In the meantime, I was not at school—waiting for the missed classes to come around—and I was not working. Byron had to work overtime and double shifts for us to make ends meet. I was alone most of the time and being newly married this was not the most secure position to have been in. Byron would come home after midnight, having been away all day, and I would be wanting a lot of attention and a lot of sexual attention and he was just too exhausted for all of that. I would even dress up in the scantiest of nighties and he would come in and fall into a chair and not even notice. I became insecure and depressed and some nights would turn wild and throw things and yell at him because I perceived that he was ignoring me.

The truth be known, at this time my emotions were running hot then cold then fevered then icy then flaming then dull. I was out of control and my new husband did not know exactly what to make of it. I was down in the dumps for a long time, from July to November and December 1967. I was not in school as I did not demonstrate well in psych after Mom died. I missed getting the required 80% by 2 points and the school made me repeat the entire course. To do that I had to stay out of school for four months, go back and make up the psych, then get the courses I missed while in psych. I would graduate eight months after my class. I would be away from my husband months at a time. I would be very depressed and then hyper as hell. I was getting a review from one of my instructors and she related to me that I was excellent on the floor, my technique was as good as they had seen, if they just didn't have to hear me coming. I was considered "hyper". I would learn to hate that particular description of my demeanor.

As soon as Pop got married he was transferred to Wilmington, Delaware, so in one fell swoop I lost my family home, ties with friends, and my father. I would not be seeing him again for quite some time. I first had to finish the last nine weeks of training and get my license and acquire a job. I was so glad when the whole task of going to school was over. I packed my bags, grabbed my diploma, and ran for the car. I ended up with a job at Springfield State Hospital, a psychiatric hospital. The director of nursing knew me when I was a student. He had seen me on a bench playing a guitar and asked me to teach his daughter to play. He thought I handled that very well and told me to come back when I graduated and he would have a job for me. I did and he did. It seemed as though I had been working there forever as I was a student there for a total of six months.

I was to head up the infirmary cottage and be in charge of all somatic services in an area known as Men's Group. I was responsible for making rounds on all of the other cottages in the group and work up appointments for the Dr. that headed up the physical medicine division of that group. I would then pass meds and supervise my own cottage which had fifty to sixty patients.

I was not very confident as I had not taken my boards yet and was still signing things as a graduate nurse. At one point I was even the evening supervisor for the entire facility with its capacity of 2,400 patients and some 90 buildings and GN was still behind my name. You can just imagine how shaken I was every time the phone would ring and someone called with a problem. It was very scary, but I seemed to have handled it quite well.

I took my State Boards and found that they were not nearly as tough as they were reported to be. In fact, I was second or third out of the room with every test. In those days we had two days of testing. Five different tests were offered. They were Psychiatric Nursing, Pediatrics, Medicine, Surgery and Obstetrics. Three tests on day one and two on the second day. If you got 350 or above you passed and if you got higher than 500 you made "nationals" and could work anywhere in the United States without having to retake the tests. It took three months to get the results in the mail. If you got a long thick envelope you did not pass and this was your reapplication to try again. You only had to retake the particular test you did not pass, not all of them. If you received a flat square envelope you passed and this was your license. Byron was home when I got my square envelope and refused to open it. I just knew there was some sort of mistake. I mean I thought the test was so easy, how could I have passed it? I finally opened the thing and out came my test scores. I started to cry and Byron was laughing at me. I asked if we had $20 for me to retake the test and he asked why. I told him the numbers were entirely too high. They must have made a mistake. Everything was over 500 and that could not be right. I was such an average student how could I ace this test when I knew that there were several top grade students that were going to have to retake them? I was just jumping up and down, but as a Registered Nurse. My mother would have been so proud.

Time passed and I decided that I was going to quit taking birth control pills and have a baby. I missed a period and was starting my second month when I was racked with pain and started to bleed very heavily. I went to the bathroom to clean up and get myself together. When I sat on the toilet a violent contraction went through my body and I could feel something passing out of me with a gush of blood. I cleaned up and put on a pad and turn around to look. Along with all the blood that was in the bowl, there was a tablespoon full of fluffy pink and white material. The bleeding had stopped and the pain was no more. I had a spontaneous complete abortion right there in my bathroom. I was looking at my first child. I flushed and that was the end of that. I was bereft. There was no need to go to the doctor as the bleeding had stopped. I would just have to wait and see when I would become pregnant again and if I could hold on to it.

A couple of months went by and I missed again. I waited a couple of weeks and went to work and had some blood work drawn. I found out at lunch that I was indeed with child. I jumped up and went to find Bryon. I grabbed him and danced around and thoroughly irritated him as he did not want anyone to know at that time. I never have known why. I was bubbling over. I danced and sang and lost sleep and generally made a nuisance out of myself. There's that "hyper" word again. That is the way I was. I tended to get onto everyone's nerves, but God bless 'em they loved me anyhow.

My job was getting on my nerves or I on it's. Every day it was an argument with the LPN I worked with on the ward. The woman had been in "charge" for years and had run off RN after RN and now she was after me. Being brand new in the job and title I had no idea how to handle this problem so I went to my supervisor who told me I was the RN and she did not need to tell me anything. "Just go handle it." I was hyper and tearful and could not sleep or concentrate and this woman was just all over me. I had been pestering Byron to let me get pregnant and now I was so I used that as an excuse to get away from the situation. That and the fact that this woman countermanded one too many orders of mine. One day a man fell off a ladder in the linen closet and hit his head on several shelves on the way to the floor. I was afraid that he had at the very least broken something in his neck. I told the people there to cover him up, take his vital signs and under no circumstances move him. As he was already unconscious I knew he was not going to move himself. I then went to the phone to get the doctor. When I came back, this nurse had the aides pull this man out of the closet, pulled a blanket out and then rolled him over on it. That was enough for me. I was furious. We later found out that he had broken several vertebrae in his back. Untold damage could have been done with all the moving around, but we were lucky. I immediately picked up the phone and called the director of nursing. I told the directory of that I needed to get off the ward and do something else. I used my pregnancy as an excuse, besides, I knew that no one wanted the evening supervisory spot, so I said I would take it permanently so no one would have to rotate that spot ever again. I got it. It was a cowardly thing to do, but took me out of an untenable situation with grace and a sense of dignity. As wild as I was when I made that request I was surprised I was not turned down as being too "hyper".

As evening super I would be stationed at the hospital's main building with a beeper and a car. The campus of Springfield was large and unless you were just going across the street you needed a car to get from one place to another. I would have one Dr. at my command who came in from the outside at 7:00 o'clock PM to stay overnight for emergency calls. These could range from lacerations to IV restarts to someone ill enough to transfer to a hospital in Baltimore. The only patients we were not allowed to treat were those that were on a lithium research project. They had their own on call list. None of the doctors coming in from the outside were psychiatrists; as a matter of fact, they were obstetricians, urologists, vascular fellows and such. I met some really nice fellows on the evening shift. They had a room on the top floor of my building and usually stayed there until I called them to come and help me with some emergency. If no emergencies, then they stayed in the rooms and slept. These guys were moonlighting after all.

One such fellow was Faysal Najjar, an Iranian from Beirut, who found working with me to be a pleasure and did not stay in his room all the time. He liked my coffee and I always made sure that it was fresh and waiting for him on the nights we worked together. We became good friends and exchanged all kinds of ideas with each other about life and the world and food and things we liked to do when we were not working. As a matter of fact we exchanged dinners at each other houses. He had a typical American chicken dinner at our house and we had a huge ornate typical Lebanese dinner at his. I made the coffee. Faysal and I became close enough that there was a sexual tension between us. I could not wait for him to come in to work. I would get all goose bumped and had a thrill in the middle of my belly and would breathe hard. I had all sorts of fantasies about this man. I was seeing him off to bed one night and he started to climb the stairs to his room and suddenly turned around, grabbed me and gave me a hard kiss on the mouth. I was so taken aback that I turned and fairly ran back to my office. Not that I had not thought of this as something that would be desirable, but that I was so ashamed that I let it happen at all. What would I tell my husband? Should I tell my husband? Turns out that that was not to be the only time that that was to happen. He got me in the elevator in the hospital a couple of times. It was all so exciting and scary.

I did tell Bryon after a while; after all, I was in love with him and the truth should never get you into any trouble with those you love. He thought I was being hysterical and laughed himself sick. Faysal actually asked if I had told By and I said yes. He was incredulous and wanted to know why, so I told him. He did not try to kiss me again for a long time and then . . . One night I was getting into my car to go home and he reached in and said that in his country they fight fire with fire and planted one on me again. That was the last as he was leaving the moonlighting program. Boy did I ever miss him. We connected again years later. But that is another story.

While all this was going on I had my son Richard, the most beautiful baby boy in the world. I had him without my husband because in those days fathers were not allowed in the delivery room. I could never understand that for general reasons, but for me it made no sense as my husband was a nurse, and I was the only one in labor at that time. It would have been such good support. At least I thought so. They did allow my friend from school, Carroll, to stay with me because she was a nurse. Go figure. I cannot complain about the entire process as I was given lots of medication for the discomfort and slept through most of it. When I was not sleeping I was hallucinating. At some point the nurse shoved my knees up to my chest and yelled, "PUSH". I did and there was a whoosh and a great feeling of relief. I asked "is it a boy or a girl?" I was informed that I had just broken my water and had hours to go. Four and a half hours later there was Richard Kevin Greene, son extraordinaire. Three days after the birth I was at home alone and realized that I was not as happy about the whole thing as I had been in the beginning, crying at the drop of a hat, wanting to stay indoors, and generally feeling God-awful. Boy, was I depressed.

I was very big on breast feeding, which, for some reason really upset the hospital personnel. I decided to place Richard on a demand schedule, which seemed most natural. Just think about it, no one really eats on a four hour schedule day and night. They eat when they are hungry, so that is how I fed Rich. If he hollered for food he ate and if he slept through the night I did not wake him up just to eat something. After about two weeks of this my breasts got rock hard and started to leak, I tried to milk them, but was unable to express any milk. Richard would get hysterical while nursing and started to spit the nipple out and wail. My ducts were blocked and that was the end of that. I was devastated and felt every bit a failure. Nursing had been a great bond for me and I loved it. Now that was no longer an option and I was crushed. Just adding to my feelings of depression and unworthiness of having such a beautiful infant.

I stayed off on maternity leave from May to August then returned to work which seemed to have helped my mood a little, with the exception of when Richard started to have colic. I would do everything I knew how to do to help him then would just sit and listen with great dread in my entire being. I would even call Byron at work and beg him to help me, sure I was going mad. I ended up giving the baby fruited brandy to get him to calm down. I figured if my grandmother could use scotch with her babies I could use brandy with mine. It seemed to help, but not for long. Another failure. I am 22.

Bunky, Byron's friend that worked as an aide at Springfield had moved to Havre de Grace, Maryland, and was working as inhalation therapist at the local hospital. He wanted By to come to work with him doing the same thing. Byron had taken the LPN course at Springfield and felt confident that he would like and be able to handle this. So, we packed up and started another adventure. I was to work in the OR and he at the Respiratory Therapy Department. Neither of us ever having done either.

I interviewed and got the job with reservations from the head nurse of the OR. After all she was going to have to train me from the beginning, and heaven knows that can be a real kick in the pants. Especially if you have a numb nut for a pupil. I was scared to death. Mrs. Garaghan was a tiny wisp of a woman with a voice like concrete. If you were in trouble with her everyone was going to know it with you. Once she was so infuriated with a doctor that she threw instruments around the OR. So, I decided that I was going to learn as much as fast as I could to keep myself "under the radar." Actually I was very good at what I did and the docs liked having me scrub on their cases.

Having been married about three years now I was beginning to notice a change in my relationship with Byron. He would go "out with the boys," a lot and not come home until all hours and when he did come home most often he was tipsy or downright intoxicated. I would never know where he was or who he was with and would wait up for him in tears or sobbing my eyes out. I would pace the house and call his friends certain something dreadful had happened to him. The night he did not come home at all I was frantic. He was supposed to be at Bunky's for a party, but there was no answer on that phone. I thought he had been in an accident, was dead, or run away from me for whatever reason.

When he got home at noon the next day he explained that someone had apparently been spiking his drinks with absolute alcohol (which is odorless and tasteless) and he passed out in the refrigerator crisper drawer and that is where he was found the next day. I was too irate to see the humor in it at the time. Then there was the time I was on call for the OR and Byron went on some errand and I was called to go to the hospital and had no one to watch the baby. I had to leave him at home. I was frantic. Why did he leave and where in the world did he go? He knew full well that I might be called in. I now realize for the first time that I am married to a man that is not really there for me after all. He goes where he wants when he wants and does not have the courtesy to even call and let me know where he is and that everything is OK or even when he will be back. I felt abandoned and unloved. As I might have been a little on the wild side when I moved here I was now falling into a pit of despair. All I wanted to do is sleep and cry.

I gain a lot of weight and am up to about 185 and want desperately to lose it. I go to my doctor and he puts me on amphetamines. I lose the weight all right and love how they make me work in the OR. I am fast and accurate and am usually ahead of everyone with the passing of instruments. I am no longer depressed—hell, I'm high as a kite and loving every moment of it. I don't eat, I don't sleep, I'm Superwoman and about to crash. The doctor decides one day that I've had enough and cuts off my supply. I fall into a very dark place. I cannot eat for a while still, and cannot sleep for a while still, but am very depressed and fatigued unto death. Byron tries to be understanding, but his way of understanding is to stay out of my way. So he does. He plays softball, goes bowling, goes to parties without me (this would become a pattern), he arranges to work overtime.

Somewhere along the line, By decided that if he was going to do this business of respiratory therapy he should have more education. So, he got himself a position at York Community College to take a course. I in turn got myself a job working at Osteopathic General Hospital in Lancaster, Pennsylvania working in the OR again. The atmosphere was much friendlier than in Havre de Grace and I saw this as a blessing. It turned out that this was not going to be my salvation as this is where my life will really start to fall apart.

I worked the evening shift which included cleaning up whatever cases were left from the dayshift and any emergencies that might come up until 11 o'clock PM at night. We would make sure that all the instruments needed for all the cases the next day were pulled and placed on a cart so the dayshift would have them all ready when needed. I was supposed to be in charge. I started out with a glowing evaluation for the first ninety days (Probation), but this was to change.

I started to have a rise in my mood, and would dress in granny dresses and "shit stomper" boots. This meant that I could not wear a bra, so I would carry it with me to work and put it on there. The only problem was I started to forget to bring it with me and would wear my scrubs without it thinking quite wrongly, that no one would know the difference. I would whiz through my work like no tomorrow and find out the next day all the things that I forgot to pull. I would mess up the scheduling for the next day. I started to have real problems with my co-workers. I began to be paranoid about everything. If I saw anyone standing off from me talking low, I was sure it was about me and my failings. I felt that they were out to get me, and I felt they did not understand my way of working or thinking and my way of doing things was the only right way. I could not handle the word "no" and would go into rages. I was not sleeping at night, but was not tired, I felt enervated. I felt that this could only be a good thing, all this energy as I was more or less the sole support of the family while Byron went to school. Oh, he did work nights driving a cab, but only brought home enough for his gas and lunch money. The rest was on me.

This high intensity energy did not last and I fell into a state of light depression during which I was diagnosed with asthma and multiple allergies ending up with ulcerative colitis. I was in the hospital for over a month. When I got out the doctor insisted that I take another 2 months off and placed me on large doses of prednisone and small doses of Valium to keep everything together. That caused great concern as I would no longer have a paycheck or insurance. I went to social services to ask for a month's emergency funds and was refused. Now we were looking at Byron possibly having to quit school until things became "normal" again. Normal was not to last as I started to bleed one day and it wouldn't stop. I had an IUD which was notorious for causing heavy menstrual flow, but this was beyond that and it was thought that I was aborting around the IUD. I was given a spinal and an emergency D&C. I was quite heavy at the time and given the position I was in it was humiliating. Listening to the doctor and the nurses talking about me was humiliating. There was no abortion and they removed the IUD. After about twenty four hours I began to have a headache which rapidly turned into the most excruciating pain I have ever had. I could not sit, stand, or lie down without this all pervasive pain. It was so bad I was afraid I would die, then I was afraid I wouldn't.

At one point things were so bad that Byron took me into the emergency room and they gave me a shot of Demerol and Phenergan for the pain. This was not all that effective. I remembered an article about headaches and ran a bath of scalding water and immersed myself into it thinking that if all the blood in my head would run into my limbs the pain would go away. Fat chance. This unrelenting pain lasted for fifteen days and I was exhausted when it was over. It turned out to be a spinal headache from the D&C. That does not turn out to be half of my trouble.

I dive into a morass of depression which is compounded by my not being able to work and the fact that Byron may have to quit school because of my illnesses. I am driven to see a psychologist. I am seeing him for free as my income had reached rock bottom. The State of Pennsylvania will not keep me for a month so now they are going to see to my mental health. Being as ill as I am the psychologist recommends that I get a

Moody Blues album called "A Question of Balance" and to listen to it often. I become obsessed with its mournful themes, I learn every word and I would sob while listening to it. I become overwhelmed with the truth of my mortality and the fact that I and the rest of humanity will surely disappear tortures me. I cannot sleep, I cannot eat, and I cannot concentrate on anything but the negatives of life-mine and everyone else's. I was bereft that my own father is going to die someday, and my son and me, and the rest of humanity. I was completely overwhelmed with la mort.

I was struggling with trying to take a nap next to Byron one afternoon. He wasn't having any trouble at all. I leapt up out of the bed, yelled at him to stop me before I did something stupid and I dashed toward the kitchen. I grabbed a serrated bread knife and ran it over my left wrist causing the slightest of wounds. Byron was right behind me and grabbed my arm just as I went for a second swipe causing a pitifully small laceration. I then shrieked and bolted out of the house into the yard. Byron went to the phone and called the psychologist and got an appointment for the next day. I stayed outside for hours with Byron close at hand watching me from a short distance to make sure I did not try any other nonsense. He was very put out and angry with me and all the "histrionics". He let me know that he did not appreciate all of this "over reacting" to whatever I thought was going on. I did not stop crying until I was too exhausted to continue and at last lay down and slept (fitfully).

The next day I was crying again on the way to see the psychologist. He started asking me questions and pushed me until I was crying so hard that the snot from my nose was running into my mouth without me caring at all. He said that he was going to suggest that I see him twice a week instead of once, but realized that I was too sick for that and suggested that I enter Lancaster General Hospital's psychiatric ward. This just made me cry all the harder and I began to wail. Byron took me to the hospital and got me admitted and was still in a semi foul humor as he felt that all of this was just so much window dressing and "acting". I was truly very ill at the time. My second suicidal gesture. I am now 24.

I spent 30 days at "camp LGH" (Lancaster General Hospital), in an open ward being treated for what was called Steroidal Psychosis. I was placed on thioridazine, perfenazine and amitriptyline, all of which were to sedate and anti-depress me. They made me feel as though I were walking in a thick fog, unable to move or think well at all. Along with the drugs there was group therapy, walks outside, games inside, and a couple of times we went to the YWCA to swim. It was noticed that Byron did not come to visit all that often and that my father did not visit at all. I do remember one visit when Byron and I turned amorous and had sex in my bathroom. An aide came into the room in the middle of everything to bring a pitcher of fresh water. We froze. When they had gone we burst out laughing and finished what we were doing. I was eventually thought well enough to go home. On the medications, of course.

When I went back to work all was not well as they saw me as a clear and present danger in the OR. So at that point, to keep me on the job, they put me into the central supply room. This is where all the materials used all over the hospital that need to be sterile come to get that way. Three of us worked there every evening, cleaning, wrapping, labeling and sterilizing the goods. What with the meds and all I was not really wrapped too tight at that time and made several mistakes in labeling. The time came when I caused another person to be hurt because of my carelessness. The tonsillectomy trays did not have all the instruments on them and after the second one the rest were to be labeled to show in writing what was missing so the nurse would know what to pull from the previous case and wash and sterilize herself in the OR proper. I had failed to do that on one case and the nurse in that room ended up doing everything in too much of a hurry and did not let the autoclave (sterilizer) vent the steam properly before putting her hands in and scalded herself. Now they really did not know what to do with me. I was now dangerous everywhere. Thankfully Byron was just about to graduate from school so I simply put everyone out of their misery and resigned. I am sure they heaved a sigh of relief.

No relief for Byron because now the onus was on him to find a job and get to work. Being very close to Havre de Grace and because they already knew him, he went there for an interview and, of course, got the job. He commuted from Quarryville, Pennsylvania, every morning and afternoon. Not a terribly long commute, but a back woodsy kind of commute and depending on the weather or time of day a rather treacherous route. He did this for a month or so then found us a house to rent in Aberdeen, Maryland, three miles from the hospital. He was now the second in command in the Respiratory department at Harford Memorial Hospital. Me? I was going to take a sabbatical as I was pooped and needed some time to do nothing at all. No work, no doctors, no hospitals, no craziness, and no illnesses although I did remain depressed it was not a matter of life and death any more.

I had a fight with Byron one day and he made it very clear that I was quite useless around the house and in his life. Without thinking about the consequences I packed a bag and headed out to the highway and started to hitchhike. I was going to go to my grandmother's in New Jersey. Problem was I need a ride over the Susquehanna Bridge. I turned down several rides as they look unsavory and took the ride offered by a clean cut looking young man. My mistake. He raped me and left me at the side of the road. The next day I got home to find Byron there as he could not go to work because he had to watch Richard. I threw myself onto my knees next to where he was lying on the couch and told him what had happened. He looked at me and started to laugh as he said, "You got just what you were looking for didn't you?" I was devastated and knew at that moment that whatever we had together in the past was certainly gone now. I mean HE LAUGHED AT ME! RAPED AND HE LAUGHED AT ME!

I had myself checked out by a gynecologist and he found a small laceration on the inside of my labia and made the remark that it must have been one hell of a wild session. I told him it was not my husband and he made the remark, "Oh then, you've been a bad girl." In my shame I remained silent. I never reported the incident to the police because of that, nor did I ever go back to that doctor. I was depressed again.

I did do nothing for ten months. Then I found out that Byron had not actually been working all the over time that he claimed. He had been going over to his secretary's apartment to do whatever they did while he was there. I knew this because I called him at work and he was not there. I confronted him that night and made him tell me who he was seeing. I then got on the phone and made an appointment with this woman to find out just exactly what it was that she was giving him that I was not able. She told me that he came there to unwind as it was quite impossible at our house. That he was stressed out because I was not working. Well, all he had to do was tell me.

I had a job the next day and started the next. The one thing I learned about my husband is he never ever confided in me. I never knew what he was thinking, what his dreams were, what he wanted out of life, what he expected from me. He would just hold everything in until he ended up angry and wanted to fight.

My new job was in a nursing home as the night supervisor. Being up all night had its effect on me and I became high as a kite. I was loud and obnoxious, and "no" was not a word I understood. I was always ready to pick a fight, and I wanted to confront this woman again as I found out that my husband had been out with her that night. I picked up the phone at the desk before report and rang her number and in front of everyone blasted her and railed at her and threatened her life. The next day I was given two weeks off to get my act together. I went to a doctor and he diagnosed me with "agitated depression" and put me on chlorpromazine and amitriptyline. I needed the entire two weeks to get used to the sedative qualities of these drugs. I slept a lot. It was obvious that I would not be bothering anyone for a long while. Even so, underneath all this medicine I was riled. I didn't actually relax for four months.

There was a month of seeming "normalcy" then I found myself awash with depression again. This lasted about three months and then another short lived "normal" state until after my grandmother died at 86 years of age. She was a wonderful woman that rarely smiled and almost never laughed, but told the greatest stories. I was to miss her most of all of the family I had lost over the years. At this point my Aunt Suzy who had already disowned my father now disowned my brother for some perceived wrong to my grandmother. My brother could be a real son-of-a-bitch when he wanted, but I could not believe he would do anything deliberate to my grandma. But, out of the family he went. Now I was the only remaining Sherman.

Working nights as supervisor knocked me out and I had to sleep during the daytime even when Richard was home. When he was 7 he came and woke me up and told me he had blood in his "bowels", so I rolled over and said that's nice dear. Later I woke up and went to the store to buy meat for dinner and when I came home he repeated what he had said and added that it was still in the toilet come see. I went silently to the bathroom never suspecting what I was to find. The entire bowl was filled with bright red blood. It was everywhere. The place looked like an abattoir and I was instantly super alert and on the verge of hysteria. I rushed to the phone to call Byron at work and find a pediatrician to see Richard right away.

The one doctor I wanted was out of town and it was recommended that I call a Dr. Shin. He took us right away and after he examined Richard recommended that we take him to Franklin Square Hospital right away, so we raced down the highway and got him admitted. When giving the history I let the resident know that I had ulcerative colitis could this be what we were looking at with Richard? The response was, "No, no, not possible in a boy of 7 years." I re-described the carnage for the doctor, but he was not impressed. Instead he ordered some tests and left the room. Rich was to have a barium enema the next day. The test was inconclusive and his bleeding had stopped so he was discharged on the second day. He came home with a very disturbed mother.

True to form a feeling of ill came to the fore with Richard coming to me again with the same complaint of having blood in his "bowels". The scene was out of Texas chainsaw massacre and back to the hospital we went. We ended up staying there for 35 days with countless tests and needle sticks in this poor 7 year old. It got to the point that when they asked Rich to go the nurses' station he would start to wail—that is where they did all the needle work. One nurse actually got nasty with my child and chided him for being such a baby about the whole thing and I almost made her eat her words. It's a wonder there was no restraining order sent out after me when it was all over. I really wanted to club the bitch. My lord, he was only 7 and in the hospital for over a month, what was it this woman expected? They were taking blood from his hands and wrists and feet two and three times a day. Be real! Then they did a colonoscopy and as they could not define what they were looking at they sent specimens to an expert at Johns Hopkins Hospital and another in France. And what was the consensus of opinion? Well, for lack of a better definition they all decided that they were looking at . . . ? YES! Ulcerative colitis! The mother was RIGHT AFTER ALL! So, what was that all about?

Byron and I had spent our vacations in that hospital. We watched the Olympics from my son's room. It seemed that we were there forever. When we both went back to work, I would come and stay with Richard until afternoon nap and Byron would get there for evening visitation. That way there was always someone there for him every day all day. Poor little guy, he was so sick. And I was so depressed. Anyway, a hand full of pills and some rectal foam and a diet and my son was finally let out of prison. When it was all said and done, I had made it to 30.

Byron had been complaining off and on that he thought that I was too heavy. He was starting to sound like my mother. At 235 he had every reason to be concerned, so I went and signed up for Weight Watchers. I went every Monday with some friends of mine and lost weight every week until I had lost a total of 100 pounds and weighed in a svelte 135.

I was now in a size 9-11 and 36-26-36. And hot-hot-hot. I was ready to roll. Byron did not seem to see the difference at all. He never mentioned it, he hardly ever touched me in any way. He still ran off with whomever at any old time and stayed for however long. The marriage was falling apart that the seams. So, of course, this was the time that I chose to show myself. I decided to run with my new looks.

Losing the weight I became to understand the power of a beautiful body and if my husband did not want it I just knew there were men out there that would. I was working at Fallston General Hospital now and meeting some very interesting men as patients and visitors. I ended up dating one of my patients and with no shame at all went to bed with him. We went to movies, rafted down rivers, even took a trip to Williamsburg, VA for a weekend. I did not even care that my husband would know this. It served him right for ignoring me. I ended up in the hospital there with my asthma and Byron had to come and get me to take me home. He thought that I got sick so I would not have to go to bed with this man. That I had an attack of conscious. Little did he know. This was not the platonic relationship he thought it was.

I was so hot to trot that I would dress at the hospital and go to bars after work knowing that someone was bound to buy me a drink and ask me to go somewhere "quiet" with them to have sex. I was theirs for the night. Buy me a drink and I was theirs for the night. BUY ME A DRINK AND I WAS THEIRS FOR THE NIGHT! I wanted sex 24 hours a day. I could not get any at home and I could not get enough, so I went looking for it any where I could find it. Thank God this was before the days of AIDS and other nasty diseases because as promiscuous as I had become I would be a dead person today. I had sex in cars, bathrooms, sheds, living rooms, motels, hotels, standing up, lying down, on top, on the bottom, on my side orally, anally, I didn't care. I just "needed" it all the time. I masturbated every chance I got.

Keeping the weight off became just as much an obsession as the sex. If I was not thinking about sex I was thinking about what I was going to eat that day. If I changed anything, what could I substitute and if I ate this much I have this much left. I overheard Byron telling someone that this really needed to stop that I had become anorexic. Even the doctor tried to make me stop as I would have one asthma attack after another now that I had lost so much weight. I even had a bout with diaphragmatic pleurisy while I was so thin. To fat, too thin, MAKE UP YOUR MIND.

We were about to move again. I counted the moves in this marriage and they were considerable. We started out in a 10x50 trailer, moved to Westminster to a small townhouse, then to a house in Havre de Grace, on to a federally subsidized apartment in Lancaster, and then to a small house in Quarryville. We rented a house in Aberdeen, then the house we were in when I lost all my weight and got crazy in Havre de Grace, down the street to a duplex still in Havre de Grace, and finally to a house of our own also in Havre de Grace. Not to call for confusion, but I just thought it would be nice to know that we moved nine times in thirteen years. Nothing like a little continuity in one's life.

So, I lost all this weight and I became manic and promiscuous and things just tended to go from bad to worse. I was now working in the same hospital as my husband only I was on the night shift. I met a security guard that made it very clear that he liked me. He took me to breakfast one morning and from there it became obvious that we were going to have an affair. I allowed this man to bed me in my own house one afternoon, never once thinking of the ramifications. I wrote about it in my diary. I wrote how he touched my breasts and held me and whispered to me and did other things that my husband used to do, but had not for such a long, long time. I wished it to be so on paper. You see, I still thought that I loved my husband and was beginning to equate sex with love. I had never had an orgasm with any other man, but my husband. I equated that as my love for him. A week or so after this tryst with this man I noticed a difference in Byron's lovemaking. Everything I wished for in my diary was there so I said something. He admitted to reading my diary and I was aghast. I cried and wailed and stomped my feet and tore my hair—guilt will do that to a person. He told me that he did not mind my having sex with this man just why did I have to have done it in his bed. He wanted me to keep it out of the house. I continued to rant and rave that if he loved me he would not want me doing such things with another man. He then asked me what I wanted from him and I told him I wanted him to tell me "no more". I wanted him to tell me to stop. His answer to all of this was, "I'm not your father." Oh, my (sigh). I should have known right then that it was just a matter of time. He had decided that we were to have an open marriage and go our own way with our own people.

He would come home in the evening and have dinner and sit down to watch TV or do the crossword puzzle in the paper. He would be quite settled when he would get up and start taking a bath and getting dressed. "Oh, I forgot to tell you there's an Orioles game and a bunch of us are going, don't wait up," and out the door he would go. Or same scenario and it was a party to which he had not invited me. Or as one night he told me right out he was taking a girl to the movies. I was so depressed by all of this that I sat down and drank myself unconscious as I could not get myself calm enough to sit still or go to bed to sleep. The next day he was so angry he lit into me with both barrels. Who did I think I was? He had come back from his date and "wanted" me, but he could not get me to wake up. "What's with that? I can't even wake up my wife when I want her?" It occurred to me that this man had gone out with a woman, got himself all turned on, did nothing at the time, then came home to his wife to spend his energy on her. What does that make her? Was I like a convenience to keep him from doing something he felt was morally wrong? Then why was he putting himself in such a position in the first place and what kind of whore did he take me for? Such sanctimonious musings for a woman that for almost a whole year threw herself at anything in pants. I hit the depths of depression yet again.

Somewhere along the line I decided that I was now too old to risk another pregnancy. It plagued me that after 30 years of age birth defects go way up and I knew I could not handle that, so I had a Tubal Ligation. I found out a couple of years later that Byron had a vasectomy without telling me and with us not having sex it would have been the easiest thing for him to hide. I found out by a doctor asking me how Byron was and I responded that I didn't know that he knew him. "Oh, yes. I did his vasectomy not too long ago." I was wild! The doctor tried to cover by assuring me that he probably made a mistake and it wasn't him at all. I knew though. You can tell when someone is back-peddling on something they have just let slip. I was now sure that the trouble was just beginning and the end was drawing very near. This meant that Byron was no longer going to use his wife for sexual release, he was going to go all the way without hesitation.

Having been subservient to my husband for all these years I decided to go off and do something independent for a change. I sent an application to Antioch University to get my degree in the humanities. I got myself a student loan and started that September. I went in the evenings and went to work at night doing my homework there as was possible. I was having myself a good time. I was like the oldest person in the room and one of the brightest. I demonstrated in every class and received 15 credits by semester's end. I also bedded the bartender at the bar down the street and one of my classmate's brothers-younger-so much younger. I was flying and loving it. However, disaster was awaiting me at home.

I was going through a box on Byron's dresser that had jewelry in it. There was an amulet that we both wore and it was in this box. What I found, however, knocked me to the ground. It was a small sheet of paper carefully folded with a poem on it about "love like butterflies must be free." A love note from a letter "D". Byron was at the duplex we had just moved out of. He was "cleaning up". So I meandered over like I was going to help him, all the time figuring out how I was going to broach the subject. "D" was Dee, a woman, a nurse that worked at the hospital. He had been seeing her for quite some time now and she had written this little note—it did not mean a thing. I knew just exactly how much it meant when he came tearing into the house one day with his finger pointed at me yelling that he had just come from the urologist and had herpes and I had given it to him. I was flabbergasted. I had never had herpes and to prove it I went back to the doctor I saw when I was raped and talked with his partner. He looked over my records and told me straight out, "Patti, you don't have herpes now and you did not have herpes then, you've never had herpes—YOUR HUSBAND HAS BEEN DIPPING HIS WICK!" I asked him to put that in writing and I flew across the street to the hospital and shoved it into his face and told him he could sleep on the couch from now on. He did not get it from me so it must have been one of his floozies. The fool told on himself.

I had been self-medicating myself with large amounts of vodka for quite a while as all this was happening and it got away from me. I drank almost an entire 5th one morning trying to get dull enough to sleep and apparently blacked out. I was lying in bed and a voice woke me up calling my name. It sounded like my mother's voice. Then I heard a man's voice that I did not recognize repeatedly calling my name. After awhile I heard Byron's angry voice shouting about the mess in the house and who was going to clean it up and what are all these notes all over everywhere. I staggered out of bed and with blurred vision and vertigo went around the house to find these voices and found instead multiple suicide notes. One of them pathetically charged that the dog slept with me more than Byron did. The notes started out legible and passed on to semi legible to scrawls of nonsense over the whole piece of paper. I was in real danger here. I denied everything to myself and only told the LCSW I was seeing on a semi regular basis.

Next in the increasingly depressing saga came the statement that he needed his "solitude" and would be taking off for the weekend to get himself together. This 'solitude' thing was not new. A lot of times he would say that when he was going out without me. Once he went to the shore for some "solitude" and came back in the middle of the night. The next day he was sporting a brand new silver pinky ring. Anyway, he packed a bag and put it into his car and was going to pick it up after the day's work. I went out to the car to get a couple of tapes to play while he was away and found a box with a hat in it along with a note that said, "While you're up this weekend we can . . .". He never did learn to hide things from me very well. He always put things in places that he knew very well I might go to get something else. So, he went on his weekend. But not until I went through the entire car to see what he was taking with him. As he had herpes, I looked for condoms and found two. I very carefully punctured each one with a needle. Hey, "all's fair . . .".

When he came home he came over to me sitting in a chair, fell to his knees and cried that he still loved me, but he could not continue to stay with me. The man was sobbing and I took pity on him and stroked his hair trying to soothe him and calm him down. The whole time I am so shocked that I was almost numb. I did not know what to do or what I was supposed to do. I just wanted to go hide somewhere and bawl my eyes out, but I sat and soothed this son-of-a-bitch. He said he was going to go, but he still slept in my bed. He said he could not live with me, but he was still in the house two weeks later. He said he could not live with me, but he was still sleeping in my bed. I was so confused I didn't know what to do.

While he was still in the house I figured I still had a chance. He wanted meals at a certain time and there they were. He wanted the house cleaned, the dishes and the laundry done, so they were. He wanted things ironed so they were. He came to me one day and said that this was not going to work that I was tying "too" hard. All right we'll try something else. I sent him a man's bouquet of flowers in an owl vase. I did not sign it just to see if he would figure it out and bring it home or if he would think it was from her and not bring it home. Second choice. I asked him about it and he made up a story about not being able to bring it home because la-la-la-la-la. It came home the next day.

I was sitting in the living room watching "Jane Eyre", while By and Rich ate their dinner. It came to the part where the little girl in the orphanage dies and I began to cry and become agitated and then angry as hell whereupon, I picked up this vase of flowers and threw it with all my might at Byron's head. I missed and it hit the wall next to his head with a mighty crash. I was right behind it shrieking and howling, my hands out claw-like with every intention of gouging this man's eyes out. He grabbed me by the arms and set me on the floor where I continued to sob and wail. I kept crying out, "Stop me, please stop me." He was yelling at me to "Settle down". Richard ended up in his room and Byron left the house leaving me on the floor rolled up in fetal position moaning for help.

One sleepless night I threw him out of my bed to sleep on the couch. He went without a word. I lay there and got more and more worked up until I got out of bed, made my way to the kitchen, picked up the chef's knife and headed toward the living room with every intention of slicing his penis and scrotum right off his body. Somewhere halfway through the dining room I realized what I was doing and dropped the knife and ran for my life. I had been seeing a LCSW for quite some time and that is where I went knowing that he would know what this was all about and how to help me. I was sobbing and hitching and fairly out of control when I got there and told him what had been going on for the last month or so with Byron. He was not very happy with him for the psychological hell he had put me through, but he called him anyway. He told him where I was and what condition I was in. Byron made the interrogatory, "What does she have to be upset about?" This social worker called a doctor he knew to get me into the hospital as I was a danger to myself. He explained I was suicidal and I had an alcoholic blackout even though I was not an alcoholic, that I was having audio hallucinations. Byron was furious, but he came and took me to St. Joseph's General Hospital psychiatric unit. A closed unit for my protection.

This place was hell warmed over. They diagnosed me with pre-psychotic syndrome—whatever that was supposed to mean. I still have never heard of it thirty years later. I do believe they made it up. Anyway, here I was in the loony bin again and on medications again and depressed with high energy again. This time the meds were chlorpromazine liquid, perphenazine, and amitriptyline. There may have been two others, but I do not recall at this time. They gave me the liquid in orange juice and it was so foul that I refused to drink orange juice for years after. This place was horrific and their idea of therapy bizarre. How did they think a person as wound up and as depressed as I was could possibly play scrabble was beyond me. Highly humiliating, I could not put two letters together and this was supposed to be therapeutic? I have to admit though, the food was great. When I was feeling a little better I asked for a day pass and went to all of the banks Byron and I had frequented and as I had packed the pass books before going to the hospital. I emptied everything out but the checking account for a total of over three thousand dollars. I then went to see Byron and as I had left a message that I would be there to visit, I expected him to be there.

He was not. Richard told me that his father had gone to the emergency room to have a laceration stitched as the cat had bitten him very badly. I waited for hours and he finally came home. I think that he thought that I might have to go back to the hospital and miss the encounter because of the late hour of the day. But there I was. I had to ask him some questions for I was confused as to what had actually happened. He had laid his head in my lap and told me that he loved me but could not live with me, then told the doctor at the hospital that he did not love me anymore and that any love that had been there simply withered up and died. How was that so? I asked him why, after he decided to leave he did not and he told me that he was afraid that I would kill myself. Then—and I have no idea what was said—he became irate and we began to fight and he hit me on the back of the head with his wrapped hand, it felt like a club. I sat on the bed and cried and he apologized to me. We went into the living room and continued to talk to one another while I surreptitiously went through Byron's wallet and checkbook. I found an entry for the apartment that we just left and I helped clean. When I questioned him about it he said, "what did you want me to do? They were going to charge me the security deposit and interest." I asked if <u>she</u> was going to be there and he quietly said yes. I went berserk and began to scream and wail and fight. We fought our way through the dining room to the bedroom where I lashed out and struck him on the arms and chest. I blasted my way through a wall and ripped out a length of wood and swung it with all my might at his head. He ducked and I smashed this board into his shoulder and he was able to get it away from me. I broke down and sobbed. I was shattered. My whole life was completely demolished. I had lost my husband, two-thirds of the household monies, my son's father, and any will I may have had to live. I was so upset that I could not drive myself back to the hospital and again a not very happy Byron was left to the task.

When we got back to the hospital I went straight to my room in tears and one of the nurses came to see what the problem was. I could barely get it out. I was ashamed for what I had done and furious for what he had done and depressed by the whole thing. All I wanted to do was to die. That, of course was not in the offing. I was allowed to stay in my room for the rest of the day with every half hour checks to make sure I stayed intact.

After two weeks I decided that I was ready to go home. I did not care at the time whether or not I was really ready, and I was crafty enough to be able to say all the right things to get myself out. Once said all I had to do is find someone willing to come and get me. I did not know a sole. Byron had kept me so out of the main stream that my list of friends was nil. The only person I knew that would come and get me was the man from the diary years ago. He was only too happy to come and get me. This was not the wisest decision I ever made, but it was the only thing I could think of at the time. This transfer was going to be interesting. I was not to go home until Byron was out of the house. Byron did not want to leave Richard until I was in the house. So, when I came through the front door he went out the back and that was that. I was home and ready to start a new life on my own. Well, not really.

Several weeks after discharge I started to get disconnection notices from cable, telephone, and gas and electric for nonpayment. As I was never allowed to do the bills and Byron took them with him when he left, I had no idea that he had not paid them for over three months. I was humiliated, furious and scared to death. I was so glad that I had taken all the money out of our accounts. I used it to make all the necessary payments.

I was not totally out of control, but very close to it. I continued to self medicate with vodka, drinking a tumbler full in the morning so I could sleep—I worked night shift—and if that didn't do it then I would drink another. I also started to use marijuana every now and then to keep it together. I had some prescription pain killers so I used them too. I needed something to keep me down and allow me to relax and feel "normal". I had been doing this when we were living together in the duplex before this house. I would take a small amount of injectable Valium or Vistaril in a syringe and take it home with me and inject it into my thighs so I could sleep. I have yet to figure out how I could do such a thing and how I ever got away with it. I was desperate, this is obvious now, but how desperate I would not know for years.

There came a time when Byron wanted to take some things out of the house. He did not let me know he was coming, he came at night, and he came with a friend. I opened the door and he pushed past me and into the house. I was instantly on alert and pulled a baseball bat out from behind the sofa screaming over and over, "Get out of my house!" I brandished the bat as if to strike and his friend took it out of my hands and held it to my face. Byron ran up the stairs and I charged up behind him hysterical, shouting over and over, "GET OUT OF MY HOUSE." He started pulling linens off the shelves and I tried to stop him by pushing him away, he then countered by shoving me down hard and I hit the ground and my head against the bedpost of the bed in the third bedroom. The next thing I knew I was struggling to my feet. I could hear the two of them in the kitchen pulling out pots and pans. I went down the stairs as quickly as the dizziness would allow and went into the kitchen just in time to see Byron pull out one of my mother's old pans. I ripped it out of his hands and told him he could not have it as it was my mother's. I then lifted it up as high as I could to get one good hard swing with it to his head, but he saw it coming and batted it out of my hands. I then picked up the chef's knife and pulled it back as far as I could, but at the last minute put it down on the counter. This man was not worth dying for. However, he saw what I intended and when the knife was down he turned on me and with his fist threatened me. I yelled, "Go ahead and hit me, you son-of-a-bitch. You like to hit women so go ahead and hit me." He did, full fist as hard as he could right in the left eye. I went down again right to the floor. I did not even remember landing. When I woke up again they were in the living room taking large pieces of furniture. I came at Byron again this time bare handed and he took the table he had in his hands and brought it up over his head and came after me. At that point I turned to flee and ran right through a plate glass door and with a spray of shards ended up on the front porch. I ran to the neighbors and pounded on the door screaming. I am now so far gone that I am urinating all over myself. Every time I yelled I peed and it was running down my leg and into my slippers. The police were called.

The police came and an ambulance. I was a sight, my hair wild, blood running down my arm from a large laceration, bruises coming up on my back and ribs, and one winner of a black eye with swelling. I could not stop crying and was too wild to give a proper accounting of what went on. Byron did not stay to explain his part in all of this, so the police said that I would have to go to the magistrate and swear out a warrant for his arrest. That if I did not do that they could not help me. The final damage was eleven stitches to the left elbow, blackened left eye, cracked ribs on the left, multiple defense bruises on both arms and multiple cuts from the door that did not need sutures. The scars are all still there. In more ways than one.

I called my father in Delaware and let him know what happened still crying and hitching and he cancelled his next day at work to come down and take me home with him. My divorce lawyer advised me to get out of town while everything calmed down. She also recommended going to the magistrate to sign a warrant for Byron's arrest. I did that on the way to my father's house. We packed some things that I knew he wanted to take out of the house, the TV, stereo, silver. I stayed with my father for two weeks.

While there I got a call from my neighbor saying he had called the police because Byron was in the house taking things right and left. That he could not get into the doors so he broke a window and went in that way. I called the police—all this from Delaware—and asked them to go look and please arrest the man for breaking and entering. They called back and said that he had a valid driver's license that stated that this was his residence, that he was quiet and polite and they could see no problem so there was nothing they could do about it. When I came home I asked about the arrest warrant and was told that it had never been served. This man beat the crud out of me and had never been served for his crime. I was scared to death, I just knew that he was going to come back and hurt me if he could. After all, I humiliated him in front of all of Havre de Grace, by calling the police in the first place. Our next stop was court.

If you have never been in court for any reason, get down on your knees and thank God with all your might. I was angry, hurt, confused, and just plain scared out of my wits. I heard the prosecutor and my husband's lawyer speaking to one another and I was described as an angry crazy woman who had been in and out of mental hospitals my entire life. I started to cry and had to leave the court house to get myself back together. If this was believed by the prosecutor or the judge I would have no case. As it was I was right about that.

This judge was supposed to be the hanging judge when it came to men hitting women, but there was something very wrong about the whole thing from the beginning. The man handling my case did nothing to help prove that Byron was even at the house let alone beat me silly. I had photos and they were shown only to Byron who said he did not know how all the damage was done unless someone else did it. We did not take the stand but in a rather casual way answered questions from our chairs. Byron said that I had caused all the fuss and that he did not lay a hand on me. The friend that was with him that night swore also that he did not touch me that night. I was asked about the baseball bat and would I have hit him if I had even the slightest chance. I answered between clenched teeth that I would have killed him if I had even the slightest chance—not good, this probably lost the case. Anyway, stories were told back and forth and I kept myself together by being meaner than a female hound and answering in low growling tones. I'm quite sure everyone thought I was the bitch I sounded like. The way it ended was . . . Byron got off scott free. It was thought that I could not have been knocked out and been able to remember anything. The fact that I remembered anything at all proved that I was making everything up—does that make any sense? He got away with the whole thing. Black eye, cracked ribs, bruises and cuts on both arms, and the eleven stitches to the elbow. He got off. I was amazed. Totally flabbergasted. Scared to death. You see, this meant that he could come into my house any time he wanted and do this again and what would be my recourse? Odds are none.

My poor self esteem came into play about now. I was so afraid to be alone that I was hornswaggled by a man who knew just who he was dealing with. This man told me that he like me and that he liked my boy. He lost his business and his house and came to stay with me for awhile. Knowing that I had a couple of thousand dollars in the bank he told me that he needed $2,300 to get his feet back on the ground. If I would <u>loan</u> him this money he would put a post dated check for that amount plus $500 on the fridge for me. I trusted this man and gave him the money and sure enough the check was on the fridge. He moved out one day and I happened to see the check with a line through the numbers and the words non-negotiable, account closed. I stared at that for a long time. I realized I'd been had. All my money was gone and I had no legal recourse as I did not know where the man went.

Now I felt as if my life depended on getting out of this house and to a place where there would be people around me. I went apartment hunting. I found a nice one in Aberdeen and signed the contract. I did not have the money for the deposit and first month's rent so I systematically sold everything in the house. I had two air conditioners, washer, dryer, stove, books, clothes. I made the cash I needed and took off. The rest of the things were put out to be picked up by the trash man. I was now truly on my own for the first time in my life. First with my parents then with my husband, now with my son. I was to be a single mother and I was at once depressed and frightened out my mind. I am 33.

If I had been fully aware of what was going on with my mental status I would have noticed that I was cycling every few months with short periods of normalcy in between. I was hypersexual at times and misbehaving on and off the job. I would stay out all night and come in and brag about what I had done to everyone within listening distance. This earned me a reprimand. After that phase I became depressed and did not bathe for days. At that time thinking a little perfume would make me safe to be around. My uniforms were not in very good shape, did not fit well, and were generally sloppy looking. I was very lucky that my friends understood that there was something wrong with me and that I was not really the slut I was portraying. These true friends stayed with me and supported me throughout.

I moved into the apartment with little or no furniture save the beds and kitchen table. I had thrown everything else out as used up and useless. It was a nice place, clean and large and well appointed. I was still working at the nursing home and wanted something better as the money was not enough to get by. I had to get another job. I did and worked seven days a week with no time off for the first twenty one days. I was so exhausted after that I gave myself a break and started to work fourteen with two days off. On my days off I would sleep the first day and then take Richard out to dinner and a movie. The next day we would go somewhere and do something together. As we had no money to spare we would end up going to Washington, DC and go to the museums there and see the sights. They were day trips with a mission, which I think was to see all the Smithsonian museums in Washington. We even went to the National Art Museum. I think that was somewhat boring for Richard so I got us out of there as soon as I could and we went elsewhere. I tried to be the best mother I could under the circumstances, but was not around enough to really do the job.

I would call Richard from work at a certain time in the morning to get him up and started for school and he would be gone by the time I got home. I would then go to sleep if I was able. When Richard came home, I would still be asleep. When I got up to go to work he was in bed asleep. We hardly crossed each other's path. It was like I was an absentee parent. When he was sick with the chicken pox, though, I stayed home with him until his fever went down and stayed. I did try. I swear I did the best I could. I loved that boy of mine.

Then there was the phone call that woke me up in the middle of the day. It was a policeman explaining to me that my son had been caught stealing candy bars from the Rite Aid drug store. I was furious. In the first place he woke me up and in the second he had been taught better than to take something that did not belong to him. I was in one of those states where things ended up being much more that realistic. I stormed into the store and told the patrolman to take him to jail and let him think about it a little while. He understood my anger, but explained that he could not do that for such a small offence. He saw my fury and told me that he did not know what I had in mind for the lad, but please go easy on him as he was terrified. Rich had even asked that I not be called at all as he knew I was going to be completely unreasonable.

Oh, I was easy on him alright. I was so furious that I growled that he go straight to his room and close the door. I then sat down until my fury calmed down to a small flame and then I went to "talk" to the boy. I asked him what he could possibly be thinking when he took the candy and his answer was, "I hope I don't get caught." A reasonable answer, but it just served to inflame me. I did not touch him at all for which I am proud and grateful, but I increased the decibels more than a mite and let him have it. It was amazing how many times I said the word f—. I used it as a verb, adverb, noun, pronoun, participle and conjunction. I was prolific with its use. I made my point with pointless cursing. I was very close to being out of control completely. I then started to sob and cry and hitch. I went to my room and closed the door and went back to bed and tried to get back to sleep. A little later, Richard crept into my room and crawled into bed with me and cried an apology to me. I enveloped him into my arms and apologized back. All was not right with the world, but it did seem a little better.

That fall I found out that Byron had cancelled my insurance for the car and health. I got new policies, one through work and the other through a local State Farm Insurance sales rep. It was a good thing as November 13th, Friday 13th, a little after 11:00 o'clock PM, on a full moon, I was passing through a yellow light when I saw a blue car in front of me. I slammed on the brakes, but hit this car broadside. It was as if in a dream. I was slammed all over the car and stunned. When the dust settled there was a man at my door asking if I was all right saying that he had seen the whole thing and I had the right of way. I was in no way responsible for the accident. He later disappeared. The police and the paramedics were called to get me to the hospital. They took me out of the car with a neck brace and on a back board as they thought that I had fractured one or the other. The other person was not hurt. The final damage was a brachial plexus injury (whiplash), and ulnar nerve damage proved by nerve conductivity tests. I had crushed the steering column, driven my knees up into the dashboard, and pushed my left elbow through the door like a center punch through wood. The entire front of the car was wasted. The only thing intact was the windshield and that was probably due to my shoulder harness. I was very worried about the person I hit, but they were down the road a little and standing by their car. So, I need not have been concerned about them.

In the emergency room there was some concern about my lower back as the x-ray seemed to show a fracture in one of my lumbar vertebrae. That was not to be an accurate finding. Everything else was intact. I was given some medicine for the pain and let loose. I was not able to work for two days. In that time the insurance company wanted me to come to the office to answer some questions. I took a cab and limped into the office. The man there told me he would have done everything on the phone if I had only told him how hurtful I was. I was horribly upset. I had to get up out of bed, pay for a cab, and go a couple of miles down the road and didn't have to. Anyway, he asked me what happened and I told him. He told me what the woman I hit said, and let me know that she had "a very convincing story." He did not believe that this woman was in the middle of the intersection on my yellow light. Neither did the police as I was issued a summons to traffic court. They were going to get me for speeding and failure to yield right of way even though I had a witness, whoever this mysterious fellow had been. So, off to court I went.

I ended up behind the lady that I hit in the accident when I went to the courthouse. I only knew this because the attorney sitting in front of me had a folder with both our names on it. He was trying to convince this woman to pay the fine and get out of there pronto. The witness was very plausible and with his testimony they would hang her. It would be much better to take the fine and increase in auto insurance and run for her life. She said she would have to call her husband first and check with him—she sounded like me the whole time I was married to Byron. I could do nothing that I did not check with him first. They got up and left the room to call and never came back. They called our case and no one got up so that was dropped. There was a man in the front that kept looking around and finally fixed an inquiring gaze in my direction. I nodded to him and we both got up and left. He met me in the courtyard and introduced himself. He was the elusive witness. You see the reason that the lawyer wanted this woman to give up was this fellow was an accident investigator and as one, would be looked at as an expert witness. He was going to demonstrate that I could not have been speeding and that I only hit the woman because she was out of place on the highway.

As I had taken a cab to go to court, he offered to take me home and explained things as he saw it that night. He was behind this woman when they were sitting at the light. It was indeed red. Another car pulled up beside hers, stopped and then proceeded with a right hand turn on red. Apparently she thought the light had changed and started across the intersection and that is when I saw her and slammed on the brakes, hitting her anyway. The police were going to site me for speeding as my tires were on some skid marks that were long enough to indicate a high rate of speed. However, this guy stated that what happened was that when I hit the car I spun around twice hitting the island and bounced with my wheels coming to rest in someone else's marks. My marks started exactly where I had testified I had hit the brakes to begin with. All I can say is God covered my butt with this guy. I never saw him again.

The man from the insurance company did not even apologize for not believing my account of the accident. I changed carriers as soon as that policy expired. I wanted someone to be my defender in the case of accident not someone who would tell me in so many disguised remarks that he thought I was lying. I did not sue the lady that ran the red light. My father did not understand that, but she had not done this on purpose and I was not about to cause her a lot of trouble. Too bad though, I did not have my car for well over two months, and then had to trade it in for another, and then found out how bad the damage was after all. The place that took the car as a trade-in sold it to someone in another state as the frame was bent so badly that it should never have been fixed in the first place. I had continuing medical problems with pain for over six months. Not to mention that I really could have used the money for general purposes. I think I was awarded a total of $1,000 for everything and that really did not cover much after all. But life goes on.

Things remained quiet for a few months, then it was time for the divorce hearing. We had to swear that we had not "cohabitated" for a year and had to have a witness to confirm said testimony. A schedule was made for visitation and payment of child support. Just before the judge brought down his gavel I reminded the lawyer that I was to have my maiden name back. She stood up and an "addendum . . ." Byron stood right up out of his chair—like he would care that I kept his name. Actually it was the fact that I was shrugging him off completely that bothered him I'm sure, after all, he was the only thing in my life that kept me going for many years. Shocking to say the least. I was too relieved to have it all over. The fighting and rankling the lying and the hatred. This man just wore himself out over the whole process. I, on the other hand, had stopped drinking and was sleeping at night again. And my son was behaving. His attitude about the divorce was a harsh one, however, as he was very angry with his father for leaving us in the first place and for beating me so badly in the second. These things he could not forgive. Me? I left my anger with the judge and celebrated my release. The final papers arrived two months later. ALL DONE! I am 35.

At this point I went and got a job in Baltimore in a nursing home paying more than $1 more than I was currently making. This was a boone that could not be refused. I was high again and I went in one night and shouted for all to hear about the job and how glad I was to get out of "this place". I had already handed in my resignation and felt very sure that I was safe from harm. I got an angry phone call the next day saying that I was to report to the office sometime in the afternoon. As I worked at night this could only be a termination interview. I did not go. I called the new job and said that my current job had released me early and I could start at anytime. Not really a lie, but very close to it. I worked there for about a year and got restless and took another job further down the road. I had been working there on weekends and I liked the place. The salary was higher and the benefits better. Off I went to a far more sophisticated nursing facility.

I had been on Thorazine and amitriptyline for years now and decided that I did not need it any more. I stopped it gradually cutting it in half every week then started to have problems with sleeping and memory. I stopped dropping the dosage for awhile and when the problems disappeared I dropped it again and again until I was no longer taking any medicine at all. I did very well for a while, almost an entire year without incident.

I worked with an agency for a while, then got a job with a nursing home in the middle of Baltimore as a Director of Nursing. This is a top of the line job for a nurse. I let the administrator know that I had never had this high a position before and was only a diploma nurse. He said he did not care, that I had answered his questions from the shoulder and he liked that. "No bullshit about you at all." I was now the head honcho and the buck stopped on my desk. If there was a problem in the joint I was the one who had to solve it. When I walked through the door there was a multitude of problems that needed immediate attention for state inspection. They gave me one month to sort things out. In that month I developed new systems and new chart papers and grafts and passed inspection with flying colors. The only problem was I was there from 7:00 o'clock AM to 7:00/8:00 o'clock PM and was responsible and on call 24/7. I could not let my guard down for an instant. I would no sooner hit the door at home than the beeper would go off and I would have to go back to work.

While all of this was going on I was looking for a house to buy and found just the one. It was the infamous "fixer upper" a veritable "handy man's special." And so I began to fix it up. I would start to wallpaper and do as much as possible before falling down exhausted. I would pack everything up and try to lie down for awhile. Then I could not stand it anymore and get up and get everything out again and start the process all over. This would go on for days. I did not sleep, hardly ate. I would go from twelve hours at work to another twelve hours at home with about two hours a night sleep. I was a maniac.

I grew very weary and again so hyper that I could hardly sit still for two minutes. It got so bad at work that I would fly into fits of tears and sobbing and rage that was unbelievable. I knew that if I did not separate myself from this environment that I would self destruct. I went back with the agency to take a breather. After a few months I asked to go back to the nursing home to get my benefits back. I was given my old job back.

Then I started to have problems with temper tantrums, and an inability to accept other's opinions, and a pathological aversion to the word "no". I was once reported by the facility's pharmacist for screaming at her over the phone. I tore up part of a chart because someone came behind me and did my work over and claimed it to be theirs. I was pulled up more than once and written up for my "attitude", and the fact that I was so "hyper". There's that word again. I was becoming incorrigible.

In this period of time I managed to have a series of painful muscle injuries, like a torn trapezious muscle from racket ball. I ended up on Darvocet-N and Valium and Flexeril. Enough medication to knock down a bull elephant. I went to work with this in my system for quite awhile. The Darvocet ended up being the drug of choice, with a little Tylox mixed in every once and a while to sweeten the mix. My doctor would give me 100 Darvocet with five refills. I was also taking a cough mixture with hydrocodone in it—that's a very addictive narcotic—at the tune of one pint with three refills. I was using all of this quite liberally. I was set up for an addiction big time. Almost every time I went to the doctor with the slightest twinge, one of these magic medicines would come out of the closet and I was using them every day to help me sleep or just cope.

One day I was having a lot of pain "all over" and asked if he would put me on some steroids and a couple of Tylox for the pain as we had done this before and it was very effective. He threw down his pen and yelled something about "another narcotic, the boys down town will love it and I will get another letter from the . . ." He refused to give me anything for the pain and showed me out of the office. I went to the pharmacy to renew my Darvocet and cough medicines and he had called ahead and cancelled all of my meds. I panicked. What was I going to do when everything finally ran out? I had to get more meds. I stormed back to the office and demanded that if he did not want to treat me that he give me the name of a rheumatologist that would.

I was given an appointment, but would have to wait two weeks before I could be seen. I went to work that afternoon in a frantic frame of mind. I knew that if I was not able to get some medication to tide me over that I would go into withdrawal. I had already had a taste of that and the only thing that kept me from tearing my hair out and getting a gun to end it all was a massive dose of Benadryl. It made me sleepy enough that I didn't notice the creepy feeling all over my body and the shakes that went with it. It did not do much for the insomnia or the abdominal discomfort, but that was nothing compared to the feeling of having insects marching along under the skin. Withdrawal is brutal. And all this because of a thoughtless, careless doctor.

I was out of control with fear and apprehension and started to cry and shake. I told my supervisor about the pain and that I could not get to my doctor until two weeks had passed and was in agony. Could she talk one of the doctors in the house to write me a prescription for Darvocet to tide me over until I could get to this man? Lying did not seem such a sin when the medicine was so important. The doctor was very reluctant, but wrote the script anyway and I calmed down right away. I was covered for a while. When I finally saw the rheumatologist I went through the same routine about the pain and he reluctantly gave me a prescription for Percocet. This was because I sat and actually sobbed my story out to him and made him feel that he just had to give me something. Now I was set for quite a while and would have a better chance at weaning myself off these drugs. I was to see the doctor again in a month. When I got back I was right as rain. As a side thought the doctor told me that I would no longer have to take the narcotic he wrote for me. I lied and told him I hadn't taken it all and threw the leftovers away. Of course, I had taken every one of them.

I now set out to wean myself from all the meds I had been taking. I knew that without this crazy, lazy Dr. I would not be able to get any more meds, so I would not be able to calm myself down with them so I'd better learn to do it without them. Weaning is not really a thing that you can do on your own. If you have the meds you will take them. So, when they were all gone I went into withdrawal. I would not wish this on my worst enemy. I was unable to sit still, I was nervous and anxious and unable to sleep or relax. It felt like millions of tiny creatures were under my skin and running up and down my arms and across my chest. I was frantic and unable to get a handle on my thoughts. I ended up calling in for several days at work as I was entirely too sick to go in. When it was all over I was exhausted. My mind was shot all to hell and my thought processes turned to depression and suicidal ideation.

I was on my way to work on a major six lane highway and was passing an eighteen wheeler when it dawned on me that all I had to do was turn my wheel sharply to the left and I would be under the truck and very dead. It was a sterling idea with one drawback. There were at least fifty cars behind me and the truck and in the lane on the other side of the truck. That stopped me. I remember thinking that the truck driver would not be hurt because he would be in front of everything, but all those cars behind me would end up right in the middle of the whole thing and I might not be the only one dead when it was all over. I continued on to work.

When I got to work I was shaken, but was able to continue with the daily chores of the job. That is until one of the nurses came up to me and asked about my doing something for a patient. I responded something to the effect of "Why ask me they're not my patient?" She became very angry and I responded by becoming livid and shouting at her. I realized at that moment that I was in trouble and left the floor to find my supervisor and friend. I tried to tell her what was going on and I lost my composure completely. I paced up and down and cried and sobbed and hitched. We ended up in the men's room as it was close. We had to go somewhere as we were just outside the board room and there was a meeting in there. I confided to my friend that I was not feeling very well and that I had just had a fight with one of my favorite people on the floor. I had shouted at her and acted a pure ass. I was sure that I had lost her as a friend and I didn't know what to do. I had great difficulty pulling myself together and I was a physical wreck. My makeup was all over my face and my hair stood out from my head as I was constantly pulling on it.

I was helped in getting myself a little more put together and we went back down to the floor. I went into the visitors' waiting room and my friend came in and I apologized. I told her how foolish I felt and how guilty and how wrong I was for the first statement and everything after. Could she please manage to forgive me? She did and we hugged and it was over for the time being.

The next day was very similar in its start. I was depressed and thinking about all the ways I could do myself in all the time I was on the road to work. I was so worked up by the time I got there that I did not even go to the floor, but found myself entering the psychiatric nurse's office. By this time I was frantic and near hysterical. I was frightened by the suicidal thinking I was having and the inability to turn it all off. I was unable to concentrate on anything of worth and was anxious and crying and could not stop. At that point she asked me if I had ever been diagnosed as bipolar. No. She nodded her head and called the supervisor to tell her I would not be working that night and shuffled me off to the crisis center at Sinai Hospital across the street.

Of course they were not expecting us so there was a very long wait for my turn. As we waited there was a woman there talking to Elvis Presley as if he was truly there and listening to her every word and answering her. She was happy as a lark. I was terrified. I just knew that they were going to get hold of me and throw away the key. I knew that I was crazy. Eventually it was time for me to talk with the doctor on call and I was shown to a room for an interview. There was a doctor and a social worker and I immediately felt terribly vulnerable. I was asked to describe what had been happening the last couple of days and had I ever felt like this before and if so when and what was done for it. I told them about my two hospital admissions and the medicines I was given. I started to get myself more composed as they asked me if they could have me come into the hospital that night. I panicked and told them that all I wanted to do right then was get back to work. That the little semblance of normalcy that would give me would be just what I needed. I would be just fine if I could just go back to work. I was asked if I always felt that I had to do everything myself and I said yes. With that the doctor asked me to pick up the desk and put it into the hall for him. I looked at this 1950 oak desk that weighed well over 300 pounds and asked him if he was crazy? I can't move that desk by myself. He then said why do you think that you can do everything else all by yourself? Got me. He did let me go after all and I went home for the night.

Oh, yes, I started out again the next day thinking that everything was going to be all right if I could just hold everything inside me really tight. By the time I got to work I was so distraught that I grabbed hold of another super and friend of mine and proceeded to get freshly hysterical for her. This time I ended up in the emergency room. We waited a very long time. As you may know suicide is not an emergency room priority. They did see me and they did talk with me and they did send me home—with my friend only. They wanted me in a safe environment until Monday when I would be admitted into the Psyche Ward—Mt. Pleasant Sinai Hospital. So we went home and had a bite to eat and she found something for me to wear that night and we went to bed, but not until I called my father and made arrangements for me to come stay with him for the weekend. Then I called my son and told him that he had to be out of my house by the time I got home or I would kill him. Oh, yeah, I was in great control that night.

You see, one of the many things that were getting to me were the facts that my son was doing drugs and doing poorly at school. He had even taken to stealing medication from my room, coming in at all hours, drinking until he could not stand up or understand English any more. He would have his friends over while I was at work for pot parties and who know what kinds of nonsense. If the police had ever been invited by one of the neighbors I could have lost my house, not to mention my nursing license by virtue of the host being my son. I figured he would take up residence with a friend or with his father—that he would be alright while I was in the hospital. Actually, I was too sick to think of the ramifications of throwing him out.

When I came home from my friend's house to get my things together for my trip to my father's for the weekend I found a real mess in the house. There was a hole in the ceiling in Richard's room and several holes in his walls. There was a big hole in the dining room wall. All the liquor I had was gone. Apparently instead of sitting back and thinking things through he got drunk and punched holes in the walls. In the bathroom I found a toilet paper spindle wrapped in tape with a hole punched into it—a bong for grass. This boy did not have the coping skills of a ten year old. He was never going to make it if he had to live on the streets. I could only hope that he would find a place with one of his friends or want to—and be able to—convince his father to let him stay with him. At any rate he was out of the house for now and I did not have to confront him. I did not think that I would have done very well if that had been the case.

I felt safe enough to get my things together and call my father and tell him that I was on my way. I got into the car, said a prayer for safety. That I would not desire turning my car into another as I drove to Wilmington, Delaware. I got there OK and went to my room to unpack when my sister came in to speak with me. She was going to a diving meet in Hershey, PA, and invited me to go with her. We would be gone all day and she would take me to eat afterward. I was hesitant, but had to do something with my time so I said I'd be glad to go. We started out early the next day and talked all the way up to Hershey. I was to sit on the sidelines where she could see me and make sure that I behaved. The irony of knowing that my sister was twenty-five years younger was not lost to me.

Between dives she would come over and see that I was OK and ask if I needed anything. Then off she would go and do her next dive. She took Second Place and was given a small trophy for her efforts. Back into the car and away we went back to Delaware. We ate at Pizza Hut and talked as friends would. We talked about things we liked to do and about men and jobs and the like. She was very concerned with what was happening to me and even though at the time I did not know, we were able to converse rather intelligently with one another. I felt very close to my sister then and she still feels close to me even today. I guess we bonded that day. What a nice thing for two family members to do.

The next morning I was on the road again for home. The house was still empty when I called the hospital to make sure that someone had actually made a place for my admission on the Psyche Ward. I was to go in at—and memory fails so I will guess at 2:00 o'clock pm. I parked my car across the street at Levindale which is where I worked and walked to Mt. Pleasant with suitcase in hand. I was scared as sin. I did not know that was going to happen or if they were going to get it right this time and spare me the agony of remaining in the dark as to what was really wrong with me for all these years. But, if I did not go in I was never going to know was I?

I was ushered into a very nice open area where one wall was stone and there was carpet on the floor. Opposite was a kitchen with all the amenities, stove, sink, refrigerator, coffee maker. They had coffee, tea, cold cuts, breads, and pastries. It was quite a setup. The nurses' station was behind and to the left of the kitchen. I was met by my nurse and the admission began. I was taken to my room (private—which was unexpected) and my personal belongings were checked for contraband—that would be sharp and dangerous objects, medications. They took away my curling iron and my keys and the ring they were on—a gigantic safety pin. If I needed these things I would have to get them from a nurse and sign them in and out. I was given a list of rules and regulations and a schedule of ward activities. There would be a short session with the psychiatrist every week day, also with my nurse daily, relaxation therapy, anger management, crafts, exercises and game time. They were going to keep me very busy.

After I was done with the twenty questions part of the admission I was allowed to walk around to get the feel of the place. That is when I met my doctor, Dr. David W. Goodman. My first thought was that he was so young—at least ten years my junior—then I thought how good he was going to be to look at—he was cute, but then I slapped myself in the face mentally and told myself that I was here to work. Good looking or no this guy was my only hope and I promised him that I would work like hell, always tell the truth, and be compliant. There was no medicine right away. He had decided that he was going to observe me for a while before making up his mind as to what the difficulty was and how to handle it. Of course, I did not know that was his plan of action, but I was willing to wait for however long it took. I asked Dr. Goodman if my problem could be menopausal melancholia, as I had gone through menopause at 38. He just laughed and said it was no longer on the "books". If I had such concerns he would be glad to have me examined and some tests done while I was in the hospital.

One of the therapies was relaxation. We were in a darkened room and lying on the floor with a tape playing soft music. We would tense certain muscle groups and relax them in cycles around the body. We were discouraged from falling asleep as it was not considered to be a relaxation mode. We also did guided imagery where a picture was to be placed in our mind and we were to gather it up and run with it. To feel the breezes and see the trees and touch the sky. I liked that one. It was very easy for me. We had play therapy where we would go into a room and play circle games like we used to when we were little kids. I know it sounds silly, but that was the most fun of all. We were allowed to throw off our adult mantle and just go with it. We also played Jeopardy and Bingo and other games that stimulated our memories and intellectual bents.

Every day I met with my doctor and would tell him how I was feeling and what I was thinking at the time. My doctor would analyze how well I was doing under the circumstances and how well the medicines were working for whatever ailed me. We would talk about what had happened to get me to go to the hospital in the first place, my history, and what was it that I wanted to get out of this experience. Three days into the hospitalization, my doctor told me that my diagnosis was to be that of bipolar (manic depressive) disorder. I leaned back in the bed where I was sitting and began to laugh like an idiot. Doc looked at me as if I was one. I saw the look and said, "Thank God it's not schizophrenia." I was then put on lithium carbonate, a medication used for decades for this disorder. No one actually has any idea as to how it works, but it does and it is a popular drug for this problem. I was also put on Verapamil, which is a beta blocker used for hypertension, but in this case effective against depression. I was also placed on propranolol, also used for hypertension, but in this case for tremors caused by the lithium. I was now ready to start getting better. At first these medicines made me very sleepy and droopy. As I clocked in with only one and one half hours sleep the first seventy-two hours in the hospital, I did not mind much that I would fall asleep every time I stopped moving.

Along with everything else that was happening, Dr. Goodman came to me early on and let me know that Bryon, yes, my ex-husband, called to see how sick I really was, and was I a danger to anyone. I was so shocked. Why would he care anyway? Then I remembered that I had thrown Richard out of the house in the hopes that he might migrate to his father's care. It sounded as if he had enough and wanted to know if it was going to be safe to send him back with me. Dr. said he was not going to tell him anything unless I wanted him to. Dr. said that he told him that if he wanted that kind of information that he would have to talk with me directly. I thanked him for that, for I felt the same way. It was no one's business but my own and my doctor's.

Ultimately, when it was time to go home it would all come down to did I want to continue seeing this doctor or did I want to start over with someone else. In my case that was a good question as I lived thirty-two miles up the road from this doctor's office. I decided that as this was the only doctor to know what was going on with me in all these years of misery and erratic behavior, it would behoove me to stay with him no matter how inconvenient it may be. He then gave me a packet of information dealing with hours available, phone numbers and rules of conduct. If you make an appointment, but do not show up without calling twenty-four hours in advance you will be charged for that visit. There will be no questions of a personal nature for me to him. No gifts given. If any home work is given it is expected to be done by the next visit. There was a quiet unspoken rule that you will be compliant with drugs and other therapies. I made my first appointment right then and there. I also asked Dr. Goodman how long he had been in the business. He froze and just sat and looked at me. I got up on my high horse and asked, "What? That too personal? All I have to do is look at your sheepskins on the wall and I can figure that out." I figured I had a right to know if he knew what he was doing. He sat quietly for a moment and I guess decided that the question did indeed have merit and answered quietly that he had been doing this work for five years. I knew it was not long as he looked to be about ten years younger than I was. On my way out the door, a Dr. Shine came to speak with me about my menopausal tests. He stated that, "According to your blood tests, your ovaries have decided to call it a day." He then gave me a script for hormones. NOW STARTS A NEW ADVENTURE. I am 42.

Three or four days after my discharge, I got a phone call from Byron wanting to come over with Richard to see what was going on. Could he come now? I said yes and started to get myself together. This was not going to be very easy for me. Byron was very manipulative and Richard was not much better as of late. I was going to have to be on my tippy toes to stay out of trouble. They both marched into my house as if they owned it. I stayed cool-just as I was taught in stress class. The trouble was soon coming.

"What kind of parent are you to throw this child out on the street and then go into the hospital and leave him there?"

I calmly explained how sick I was at the time and that I thought that he would be able to find a place to stay. That, of course had nothing to do with anything.

"When can he come back to live with you?"

"Any time he wants to sign a behavioral contract of how he will conduct himself should he want to live here."

"Why did you throw him out in the first place?"

I explained about the drugs—the marijuana, Percocet, alcohol, generalized theft and destruction, skipping school.

"If there were drugs in the house, where were you?"

At this point I almost lost my cool exterior, my façade, my sophisticated air and said in a controlled but gravelly voice that I was down the road forty miles making a living so this boy could have a house and clothes and food.

"Where have you been the last four or five years?

Byron continued to bait me, but I remembered that there was a difference between a fight and an argument. Byron was trying very hard to turn this into an argument and that meant that nothing was going to be accomplished. So what I did was lean up against my door frame and look down at the floor and said nothing at all. Byron was incensed by this and carried on and on with one accusation after another. One name called after another. I remained mute. Thinking he had won this round, he had Richard get some of his things, pulled him out of the house and was away. I took a huge breath and sat right onto the floor. I had never been so happy that I had taken some "how to" courses in my life. Those classes at the hospital really saved the day. I knew that Byron was flushed with victory, but little did he know that he had not won at all. I simply outwitted him by not answering back. That is when I would have lost the round, but he was unable to get me mad. VICTORY WAS MINE!

I was to see Dr. Goodman every Monday night at 7:45 o'clock pm. As I was going to be going back to work and this is right in the middle of my shift, I was going to have to make arrangements to see him then. I could not see him in the daytime as he did not have hours during the day. The higher ups at Levindale allowed me to leave work for the 7:45 o'clock pm appointment and come back after my hour with the psychiatrist was over. No penalty—it was considered to be my lunch hour.

It was strange not to see a doctor in the middle of the day. Evening hours, I knew, were not unusual, but at that time of night it certainly was. When I got to the office the first time, I was a little early, so if I got lost I would have enough time to recoup. I sat quietly in the waiting room for Dr. Goodman to come get me. I marveled at the fact that there was no secretary, no window for a secretary, that when he did come and get me that no one left the office first. That when I left there was no one waiting to go in. This happened every time I was there. I came to believe that I was the only patient that he had. I do know that his diplomas were nowhere to be seen. Someone else's diplomas were on the wall. He was borrowing the room and that is why he had all his visits at night.

On the outset I was asked to make a "Life Chart". This would be a calendar as far back as I could remember with up and down cycles noted so it would be easier for the doctor and I to see what kind of patterns I may have. Instead of the usual square calendar I made a linear one so the months lined up straight across. So much better to see the actual pattern if a pattern there be. Dr. Goodman told me that he had never seen anyone do it that way before. To make things crystal clear I put hypomania in red, depressions in black and medications in blue. I then wrote a bit of what was going on at the time to make sense of the whole thing. I was told it was worthy of publication.

It took me a long time to get used to therapy. I mean, let's face it, I had been ill for most of my life and had never talked with anyone about it. I did not know how to play the game. The first couple of visits were difficult, but he asked me questions and I answered them. That was relatively easy, but when it came around for me to decide what we were going to address, that's when it became very murky for me, especially when the good doctor just sat there and would refuse to show any emotion and did not talk very much. I got to the point where I could not handle it anymore and flew into a veritable fit. I railed him from top to bottom, told him that if I wanted to talk with the wall I would talk to the walls of my shower stall. I wanted to talk with a real live human being and this just did not fill the bill. I told him how rigid I thought he was and how much it bothered me. He thought for a moment then asked typically, "Do you feel better now?" I thought I was going to strangle the man. This pent up anger took an entire session.

Once in the beginning while he was asking me questions it was very obvious to him that I did not understand the game and he asked if I thought that he was looking for pathology. I said yes, it was a worry for me that he was looking for things to be wrong with me—as if there wasn't enough already. He explained to me that that was not the purpose of the sessions we were having. We already knew what the pathology was—bipolar disorder—and that this was what we were addressing. Knowing that made life a lot easier for me. We were not necessarily going to do any "you hated your mother or you were abused as a child stuff." That was for the psychologists and other mumbojumboists. We were going to work on the here and now until I felt like I wanted to change the subject. If that meant we would hold court to those other types of demons then we would.

When I went back to work everyone was very glad to see me and they did not treat me any different—sort of. They worried about me and if I was going to be alright, but they did not smother me and make me feel like I was a freak or crazy. I said that to the doctor once and he went pale. Crazy was not a word to use in front of him. Bugger off. It's my word and if I am using it in my direction then just bugger off. That's just a little tight assed for me. If he thought that was awful my next exploit almost gave him apoplexy. I was so glad that I finally had a diagnosis that I went to the DMV and got a license plate that said BIPOLAR. I kind of sneaked that up on him. When he finally got the idea he looked at me, leaned over and asked,

"You put your psychiatric diagnosis on your license plate?"

"Yes".

"You are the only person in Maryland to have BIPOLAR on their license plate?"

"There's no room for a 2."

"Thousands of people are going to see your license plate?"

"Yep".

"Why in the world would you do such a thing?"

I tried to explain to him that it was important and necessary for me to do this, but he was already so full of shock and dread that I don't think I got through to him. At least not right away.

A couple of years later I was through with the plate and was looking for another, so I took some pictures of the plate on my car and presented a good one to him for posterity. He was so taken with it that he put it into his briefcase. He asked me if I would mind if he showed it to some of his colleges. I told him that thousands of people have seen it on my car why in the world would I mind. You see, after a while he had become as proud of that plate as I was and had come to realize how important it was that I had it. He now uses it to teach newly diagnosed people with bipolar dx. It is even on the internet on his website with a short

dissertation about me—without using my name, of course. That was one
horror—his lean on the situation—that worked out for the both of us.
We both ended up getting a kick out of the whole thing.

Shortly after I went back to work I decided that I wanted to go on
vacation for a while and relax. I had not gone anywhere by myself since
I was eighteen and went to Salt Lake City on the train alone. I decided to
go to the shore, even though it was in the winter and off season. I figured
I could get a good room and for next to nothing. True, I could and I did.
I went for three days and two nights. I got a very nice room facing the
ocean for $116. This included two queen sized beds, a living room, and
an eat-in kitchen with everything you needed to make meals, including
plates, flatware, cooking pots and pans, even a microwave. Knowing
all this I packed a care package so I would not have to buy many meals
outside the room. I walked on the beach and boardwalk, drove down the
coastline and saw the sights, shopped for souvenirs. One of the things I
got to bring back was Ocean City's famous salt water taffy. I decided to
give some to the doctor who made it possible for me to take this trip in
the first place. I knew that I would not get way with giving him an entire
box as that would look like a gift, so I put a handful into a baggie and
went to my next session with it. Not as a gift, but a trophy on my success
in handling everything. After we were done I handed it to him. What a
mistake that was. He took hold of it with his forefinger and his thumb,
held it away from his body with a face that looked like I had just handed
him a bag of dead rats.

"I don't usually accept gifts from my patients." Still holding it away
from his body, whereupon I grabbed it with force and said, "You don't
have to be such an ass about it. Just give it back. Sorry."

Not long after this, on a Sunday, I was lying on the couch in my
underwear watching TV when the phone rang. It was Linda, my
stepmother. She was well controlled, but obviously distressed when she
told me that she had called because my father had had a cardiac arrest
and was in the Cardiac Care Unit in the Wilmington Hospital not far
from their home. Could I please get there as soon as possible. I jumped
up, got dressed, called into work, and hit the road. I was on I-95 going
north and crying my eyes out. My father was dying and I had to get there
so I could tell him that I loved him before anything happened. I really
cannot tell you how I got there in one piece as I shouted and cried and
was speeding all the way there. I had never been to this hospital before
and the fact that I had not written a thing down as far as directions

went was not a help to me. God looks after people like me so I made it without difficulty.

Pop was in the unit, pale and frail looking. He had been the patient being seen on medical rounds that morning when he started to have excruciating pain in his chest. He was put on a morphine drip, but they were unable to relieve the pain. The next thing he knew everything started to blacken and he woke up in the unit. He had his arrest in front of the entire cardiac residential service. Good timing I would have to say. After I was with my father for awhile, I came to the sitting room to let others go in. I found out there that my father had asked to have Byron called to see if he would please come to see him. What? As it turns out my father was very upset about the divorce and the abuse, but he still liked Byron as a person and it was important for him to see him now. What can you say? Apparently he was also going to bring Richard with him. It would be the first time for me to see him since I first got out of the hospital. I then got on to the phone to call the office of my psychiatrist. You remember one of the rules is if you do not show up for an appointment you have to pay for it anyway. I got a recording and prayed that my father having a cardiac incident would be a viable excuse.

Of course it was accepted and I went back the next week. Dr. Goodman was very concerned as to how I was going to handle the situation with my father and we spent our time talking about him. I had not said anything much about him up to now, but ended up unleashing a lot of my thoughts about him. I had my father on a pedestal all of my life. He is the one person that was steady and reliable in my memory. I mean, he has gone everywhere and done everything. He knew Werner Von Braun, Jonas Saulk, the cardiac surgeon Cooley, and had lunch with President Reagan. He was a well known aeronautical engineer who did research for the Navy on the Little John in Alaska—taking him away from us at Christmas one year—it made his career that trip. He was responsible for the third stage rocket motor on the Vanguard rocket—the one that had such a terrible time getting off the ground. Of course, it was not his motor that malfunctioned. It was his retro rocket that allowed the first soft landing on the moon. He was well enough known that the Japanese asked him to come to Tokyo and speak at a symposium they were having there one spring. He is super intelligent with a mind like a trap. He and I are never allowed to be partners when playing Trivial Pursuit because we always win. He knows and remembers everything.

Yeah, he's my Pop. But I always had a suspicion that he did not always picture me as his perfect little girl. I am not pretty, I am overweight, and not always so clear in the head. And now I am bipolar—not <u>right</u> in the head.

When I had come home from the hospital and visited my father in his home I brought a pamphlet with me. I think it was called "Lithium and You," a dissertation on what is meant to be bipolar, the medication lithium, and how important it was to remain compliant, labs you need to keep up, and where bipolar disorder may come from. It explains that it is thought to be genetic. Well, when Pop got to that particular part of the book, he jumped up out of his chair so fast that he knocked it over. "I HOPE YOU DON'T THINK YOU GOT IT FROM ME!" He was livid to say the least. Now I had to contend with the fact that he was going to be afraid that people were going to look at me and then look at him and think my disorder was going to somehow reflect upon him. Actually when you think about it, my mother was probably the source.

That done I decided that I wanted to show myself that I could get myself organized and mobilized to take a real trip. I went to a travel agency and got myself a trip to Chicago. I remember being there when I was a kid and I wanted to go back now that I was older and would know and understand what it was I was looking at. I got a plane ticket and a room and some brochures. I talked it over with Dr. Goodman and he was all for it. I was on Verapamil daily for the depression and had been on it successfully longer than anyone else had been. Dr. wanted to present me on grand rounds at Johns Hopkins Hospital to answer questions about taking it and how it made me feel, but that did not pan out. I had an EKG and it turned out I was in 1st degree heart block from the medication and had to discontinue it. A couple of weeks later on the forefront of my trip I became very depressed again and called Dr. and pleaded with him to put me back on the med. I cried on the phone that I could not go on the trip feeling the way I did and if I did not get back on the medicine now I would be too sick to go. He put me back onto the Verapamil.

I had never gone anywhere in a plane before—having a ferocious fear of heights and flying, but I was going to do this as proof of my recovery. I was going to fly, find my own hotel, and map out my own itinerary for my five days in Chicago. I find it amazing that I was able to do that. I stayed overnight with my father and flew out of Philadelphia.

I was seated next to a 75 year old lady who asked me if this was my first flight. I guess she could tell by my rigid demeanor and hand clutching. She told me not to worry, she'd been flying all of her life and she was still in one piece. The take off was chilling and exhilarating all at once. I almost cried out with the joy of it. When the attendants came around with drinks, one looked at me and said, "You must be Patti Sherman. I bet you could use a drink right about now. Your Dad told us this was your first flight and to take good care of you." WHAT? Turns out my father had followed me to the plane entrance and told the hostess at the door of my fear of flying. I was so humiliated. Come on, I was 42 not 4. Oh well, he just wanted me to enjoy myself. And so I did.

I was thrilled to be in Chicago and when I got to my motel I started to make plans as to where to go and what to see. One place was the Museum of Science and Industry. I stayed so long the porter was calling that the museum was closed and I was wondering where all the time had gone. I also made a trip to the Museum of Natural History. I became so enchanted by the snowy owl that I forgot where I was. I became fascinated by the tiny feathers around the beak that I leaned in and leaned in and BANG, my forehead slammed into the glass case. The sound reverberated all over that wing. I pulled away looking around hoping no one had seen me.

I spent one day meandering around Chicago admiring the town houses and going to the Handcock Building, waterworks castle and the Sears Building. Despite my fear of heights I went up to the observation decks. While I stayed back from the windows I was able to admire the view. I went to the Lincoln Zoo and was very distressed over the state of some of the animals. The areas in which they were kept were clean but exceedingly small. The animals were horribly stressed. One lion was walking back and forth and every time he turned he would turn into the wall and scratch his nose. Back and forth rub-rub. His nose was scabbed and bleeding. The primate house was even worse. Even though it was new and more spacious they had nowhere to go outside. I saw that they were not moving and one was lying on a bench with his head tucked under his chest. OH, MY GOD. These magnificent gorillas were severely depressed. I could not stand it and began to cry and made my way out of the zoo and to my motel. It was hours before I could get those images out of my mind.

For the next year most of the time I was in good mental condition. Then I began to get a little over wrought about my job and how things were changing for the worst. I would feel depressed, but had high energy. A most uncomfortable way to feel. One day I was counting narcotics before going home and a cassette of morphine was missing. Well, it had been counted 8 hours previously and should have been there. Not being as conscientious as usual I threw up my hands, told the night shift it was their problem and left.

The next day I was called to the office. It was explained to me that the morphine had been placed on a man who was to have a blood pressure med to increase his pressure. We had been lucky that we had not killed the man. I and the nurse who actually had made the mistake were written up and suspended for a day. The suspension was waived. This was not the worst. That was coming.

I came to work one day, got report and set up meds. I realized that a hospice patient that was on standard pain meds had not been given any the entire day shift. I pulled up the med, signed it out on the narcotic sheet for her next dose at 6:00 o'clock PM. I also charted it that way on the medication sheet even though it was before 4:00 o'clock PM. I wasn't thinking and it caught me.

I went to dinner at 5:00 o'clock PM and when I came back at 5:30 o'clock PM the patient's daughter was in the room. She asked when her mom got the last dose and I could not remember. As I had charted the dose ahead, looking at the med sheet and the narcotic sheet was no help. I choose a time and the daughter said she was in the room then and it has not been given. I backed up the time, but she had been there then also. I then remembered the time was right after I had got in that day, but by now my credibility was shot. I got permission to give the woman an "extra" dose and this time I gave it with the daughter present.

The next day I was pulled into a meeting of my supervisors who asked what in the world happened the day before. I tried to explain, but ended up crying and stating that I had days when I would stand in the middle of the hall wondering where I was. Now you know that was just wrong. My credibility went right out the window—again. They looked at me like I was just this crazy woman who has obviously popped her cork.

The day after this the shit hit the fan for real. I was asked into an office in the administrative wing with two women I did not know. They were loath to introduce themselves. They held up my now ten pound personnel file and started going through it. They cited some infractions before I was diagnosed and worked their way up to the present. They reminded me of a transcription error, the morphine debacle, then the incident with the pain medicine two days before. They then announced that I was terminated. I wanted something in writing. I was told that they would mail it to me. I'm still waiting. I was then escorted to the front door and the things in my locker were fetched by security while I waited there. I announced to everyone coming in the door that I had been fired without being told as to why. They were horrified. Now I was in a panic.

I was in the car and on my way down the road home when it dawned on me that these idiots thought I had run off with that first dose of narcotics. That instead of giving it to the patient that I had somehow found a way to give it to myself. What with my strange behavior in the one meeting and backing up the time until I got one when the daughter wasn't there—well—I guess that's just what it looked like. I started to cry. I had to get to Dr. Goodman but fast.

I called and got an emergency appointment for early the next day. I sat on the couch boo-hooing about the administration thinking I had taken the medicine and what was I going to do now. He listened and was supportive, I guess, after all he knew that I was not an addictive sort of person now and would never have taken the drugs. I felt better after—I guess. Now I had to get down to the business of getting another job. I was rather leery about whether or not this episode was going to follow me.

I had worked with an agency before and I called to sign up again. I ended up at Church Hospital. The supervisors respected my work and I was called to the office with my calendar to fill up with shifts to work. I was working full time and better and making money had over fist. I did this from January to April when I was told the hospital was getting rid of all agency nurses and would I please come on board. Well, the pay was ten dollars less per hour, but the benefits were far greater. They even offered me a $3,000 sign on bonus. What's not to like—I signed on. So now I had a permanent position, a health plan, a 401K and guaranteed full-time work.

I made friends at church and let them know I was bipolar so if I was having a bad day they would not get over anxious about my behavior. My doctor questioned whether or not this was a good idea. I assured him that it was to my advantage. I was quite the advocate for bipolar dx. My workmates always asked me about patients that came in with the diagnosis. They became very educated on the subject.

As far as education goes, Johns Hopkins had and still has an annual symposium of DRADA—Depressive and Related Affective Disorders

Association. They would present science projects, family point of view, affective disorder in history—Beethoven, Lincoln, van Gough. Then the highlight of the day is an actual person with one of the affective disorders giving their point of view. Some are known celebrities. My first was Dick Cavette. He related how his depression manifested and he handled it and how he's handling things now. These very special people were interviewed by one of the researchers at the "John".

After a few years of attending these meetings, my doctor started to encourage me to write a book so I would be able to be invited to a meeting where I could be interviewed. I fooled around for several years and finally started this book. I brought the first forty five pages to him, but found out that after a few months he had not read any of it. I quit writing. I figured that if he was uninterested so would everyone else be. I put it up for two years.

I've always been intrigued with tattoos and now that I was older I could get one with impunity. I started with a dragon on my left leg. I was probably a bit high at the time, but as I collected the beasts it would be a good place to start. I was able to handle the entire procedure without any problems and so decided to get one on my chest. This was more celestial with the sun, moon, stars, and the solar winds. Not a wise move. The pain was so intense that I almost fell out of the chair. My vision went white it was so bad. I had to call a halt and come back to get it finished. From there—who knows—I ended up getting bracelets on each of my wrists. I am ever so colorful now. Patients and visitors will exclaim their like of the tats that show. If I'm in the right mood, I will show the ones that don't. That's where I stopped. My doctor just shook his head. I am 46.

The next two years I was up and down. Not severe enough to go to the hospital, but enough to have to take time off from work while we messed with my meds. I had started with lithium and verapamil and gained fifty pounds. Being on lithium my thyroid was subpar. We did the test and my doctor decided that it would be a good thing to come off the lithium to see if my thyroid would start to work again. I was put on synthroid to boost my thyroid and I lost those fifty pounds without even trying. Now no longer on the lithium, I was placed on Depakote. For three years I got higher and higher. The Depakote was not holding my mood in check anywhere near as well as the lithium and I started to demonstrate to my doctor. I had "glamour" pictures taken after I lost the fifty pounds when I stopped taking my lithium. Leather and cleavage all the way. I took great pains to show these to my doctor. I was getting somewhat hypersexual and flaunting it in the doctor's office. It did not have the desired effect, so as I was now so uncomfortable with the almost constant hypomanic state I'd been in that I finally jumped up and down on the man's desk. I had not taken the lithium for three years and it's time had come. I told him that I did not care if I ended up weighing 500 pounds I wanted my lithium back! He looked at my file and uttered "The Depakote really hasn't been holding you very well has it?" I took home a script for lithium and in a few weeks was feeling much more in control.

Work was not really a problem, but sudden changes did affect me profoundly. One night I was not feeling so well and was pulled from my floor to another. I stood by the med cart on that floor getting more and more apprehensive, anxious, and agitated. My mood crashed and I started to cry, then sob. I called the supervisor and she invited me to her office. I sat at the table and wept. I leaned over and repeatedly banged my head against the table. The supervisor calmly helped me get more or less together and sent me home on the promise that I would not hurt myself and that I would call back to let her know I got home in one piece. Did both and was off for two weeks.

I had a cat named Mittens because he was polydactyl (had extra toes on his front paws) and looked like he was wearing mittens. One day he came into the house looking very distressed and in pain. He was unable to sit down. I took him to the vet and found out he had a subluxed tail (dislocated) and a fractured lumbar vertebra. The injuries were apparently caused by someone picking the cat up by his tail and slamming him into a tree. Halloween was not far off. This looked like a malicious gesture by some kids. Who knew. Mittens slowly, mended and one day went out and never returned. I was bereft. Then I was pissed. Someone took my baby and was doing God knows what to him.

As the days went by I started making flyers to put on poles in the area. I described the cat and his wounds. Nothing happened. I was furious, anxious and getting higher and higher moment by moment. I finally made a DEAD OR ALIVE posters with graphic details of his wounds and offering a large reward. A counselor at the middle school called me and asked if the posters were on the level or was somebody playing a gruesome joke on me. "No, they're mine. I wanted to shock whoever had the animal to call me and give him back. Dead or alive."

I was sitting in my living room watching TV when the kids started passing by on the way home from school. I had stapled a flyer on the telephone pole opposite my house. A young boy pulled the poster off the pole and threw it into the air laughing and dancing. I leapt up in a rage and flew out my front door no coat and no shoes—it was late November. I ran towards the child screaming incomprehensively about the cat and did he have some information. He said, "It's only a cat." He said something else smart. Brimstone coursed through my veins. I exploded and screamed, "I hope someone does to your mother what they did to my cat."

At this point the young man is on his back on the ground with me hanging over him. "You think you're so smart. I have a rifle in my house and if I bring it out here you won't be so smart then will you? Just let me know how far you want to take this?" At that point I turned and ran back into the house, slammed the door with my back against it hyperventilating. I realized I was out of control. I had just threatened an eleven year old with a gun, for God's sake. I picked up the phone and called Dr. Goodman for an emergency sit-down. Having explained what happened to the doctor, I took my prescriptions home and called into work. I was to be out for at least two weeks to get the meds working and me to get things together. I've sorta made it to 51.

I was at Church Hospital for ten years. During that time someone asked me where I would go if I could go anywhere I liked. Egypt was my immediate reply. Later I thought about that and said to myself, "Why not?" If I get crazy over there, I was sure that I would be able to get help somewhere. So, I went to a travel agent and pursued the possibility of going alone to the Land of the Nile. I started packing four months early and people thought I was crazy. I would then remind them that I had papers for that. I just did not want to be 6,000 miles away from home and not have something. Going to Chicago was one thing, but this was going to be a great challenge for me. I made lists and lists of lists. Packed and repacked. Got a journal, checks, passport. I was almost obsessive in my organization.

I got there. I saw such wonderful things. I made close friends with the guide who showed me a lot of positive attention. I spent money I didn't have and didn't care. I felt safe and secure and got home in one piece. I will never have such an exhilarating time again. I learned that traveling alone is the way to go. You don't have to worry about holding someone up or being bored with something someone else wants to do.

All my trips from then on would be alone—western Canada and Greece, the shore.

Church Hospital, eventually it was sold to Johns Hopkins Hospital and we all had to find another place to call home for the remainder of our careers. I chose Good Samaritan in Baltimore. They had a unit there that catered to people, mostly orthopedic surgical, that needed a gentler more friendly form of rehabilitation. I interviewed and fell in love with the place. I was to work my usual nights, but before I could start, the Director of Nursing called and asked me to do a great favor. I was to work eight-hour evenings doing all admissions for the floor. There could be anywhere from one to five and they would all be mine. I was required to transcribe the orders, call the doctor and get them verified, interview and assess the patient from head to toe, write a note and give report to the nurse that was to receive the patient. The first couple of patients took over two hours to complete. This was never going to work unless I figured a way to get things done in a more timely manner. Five patients would end up taking over ten hours at that pace. Bipolar or no, when stable I had great organization, prioritizing and delegating skills. I cut my time to a little over an hour.

Eventually I was needed for twelve-hour night shifts so off I went to the shift I was hired for in the first place. I was stable for a while and then started to get hypomanic (high). While high I met and flirted with a fellow on the IV team. I met him when I was pulled to the floor across from mine. He gave me a lot of attention and I flirted right back. He gave me his telephone number and his e-mail address. He asked me for mine and I gave it to him without hesitation. Higher and higher with more and more hypersexual behavior showing itself to this man. The first time he called me we talked until the battery on my phone went out. The next night we spoke until the early morning. Then we started meeting at work.

He did not want anyone at work to know that we were fooling around, but came to my floor to talk. Once during a mock code—staged cardiac arrest—he came into the room and quietly grabbed my buttocks. I jumped and folks took notice. We necked in his car, the hospital library, every elevator in the hospital, the second floor bathroom, my car. On my birthday he came to my house with a bottle of wine and we watched a movie before bed. In bed, we went wild. Every position and every orifice. I should have been spent—he was—I was still high as a kite and my good senses were gone with the wind. We would play sex games on the phone. He insisted that he always knew when I had an orgasm by the way I was breathing—actually I never did have any—but would play on.

I was erasable and having "fun". I talked to my doctor about this man and how he was keeping me up all night—a real no-no. If you don't get enough sleep your brain becomes mush and that was where I was headed. I asked the doctor not to ask me to give him up as I was having too good a time. The good time started to tarnish. My mood was now labile and often mixed. I became so ill my doctor recommended the hospital. I was severely depressed with high energy. An ugly situation known as a mixed state. As the hour was late he made me enter a contract that I would wait for his call the next day with admission instructions and do myself no harm. I promised.

I was up all night and flying the next day. I became morose, went into the kitchen and plucked out a butcher's knife. I played with the idea of slashing myself when I slipped and cut my thumb. It hurt. I put the knife away. The doctor called and was having difficulty getting the insurance company to OK the admit. The fact that I was able to enter into a contract with the doctor made them feel that I was not that sick and they would not accept the fact that the doctor felt it was imperative that I go to the hospital. I hung up and waited some more. I started to cry, sob, and pace. I was losing my sense of perspective. The doctor called back and asked me a bunch of questions having to do with how I was feeling now and what did I think I needed to do right now to protect myself. I got quite hysterical and said, "What do you want me to say? That I want to kill myself right now? That I cannot do this anymore?" He then asked me to hold tight, he would be back to talk to me again. "Just hold tight!" I waited awhile and the urge to just get it done overwhelmed me. I went to my bedroom closet and pulled down my Ruger semi-automatic 22G rifle. I examined it up and down, in and out. I took down the cleaning kit and cleaned the rifle in and out. Having made it sparkling clean I began to figure out how to get the muzzle into my mouth and pull the trigger at the same time. The phone rang. Doctor was on the phone. He said two words. "Go now!"

I was four days in the hospital. They gave us coping classes. Let us into the yard a couple of times a day for some fresh air. They would not let us hang around in bed and made sure we ate. As my doctor no longer worked out of hospitals, I had a doctor I had never met. He was from South America and I knew just enough Spanish to tickle him.

I never realized how manipulative I was until then. I would say just what he wanted to hear and was discharged early. Not before spending Christmas in the hospital. Luckily I had friends at the hospital where I worked come and visit on Christmas Eve and Christmas Day. My son and his wife also came with gifts on Christmas.

I stayed home for two weeks after hospital then went back to work. I brought in everyone's presents. I was passing them out prior to shift when I was suddenly overwhelmed by a feeling of doom. A black cloud fell over me and I ran to the bathroom and started to cry. The unit secretary made me open the door and came in with me. I continued to cry until I was sobbing and quite incomprehensible. My director came in and here we are three women in this tiny bathroom and me out of control completely. She asked me what I wanted to do. She "understood" and it was up to me. I wanted to—needed to—go home. The secretary helped me to my car and admonished me to call when I got home to tell them I was OK. I did.

I called my doctor the next morning and made an emergency appointment. He took one look at me and said "hospital". So we would not have the same difficulty of the last admission, I was to go straight for a general hospital that dealt closely with the psychiatric hospital and be admitted from there. The theory was sound, but the application was not as smooth. I waited for hours and was finally seen, evaluated and taken by ambulance and readmitted to the same ward for another three to four days. I was not so cocky this time. I had learned my lesson. I behaved and was compliant. I was no longer in crisis when I was discharged, but still needed a lot of work. Ultimately I was to be off work from January to August then return to work. My doctor and I went through many medicine sessions trying to get a combination that would finally raise my mood without over kill. We went through a lot and each failure took its toll. I finally asked about decreasing availability. Would we ever run out of meds to use? He said no, but it truly worried me. I started feeling better in June. I remained feeling better into July. I was given leave to go back to work in August.

July 28th, Saturday, I went to church and then home. I was going to take a nap, but decided that as it was such a nice day I would clean out my gutters. Out came the ladder and up I went. My neighbor came home and hollered, "You couldn't wait for me?" He said. He would do them for me. I responded, "what, and wait forever?" Now, we all know that God does not like cocky. I was one yard from being done when I noticed that the ladder was getting shorter. I figured that if I held on tight and kept my body flat against the ladder that I would go straight down and land on my feet. Not so. It tilted to the right and threw me off twelve feet to the ground. A sudden pain then nothing. I knew not to stand up. If something was broken it could end up pushing right through my skin. Not a problem I wanted. I rolled a couple of times so I could get away from the house and be seen from the street. I looked to my right and called, "Ed, oh, Ed." No answer. Then to my left and called out, "Ron, oh, Ron." No answer. Then straight up, "Anybody".

Ron was on his cell phone when he saw me lying on the ground. He came out of his house with his phone. "Should I call 911?" "It would be a good place to start, I think." He called and a bunch of neighbors came out of their houses. They all had police monitors and heard the address. Ed came over and asked, "What are you doing down there?" "Oh, Ed, come down here with me. I'm making animals out of the clouds." With that the ambulance and my son—called by Ron—arrived and I was off to another adventure.

Upon exam I was assured that my hip was not broken, which was exactly what I thought I had done. My leg was not shorter than the other and not splayed outward as legs do when the hip is fractured. I just told the Physician's Assistant, "Let's just wait for the x-ray, shall we, I have a feeling." When I was presented to the ER this fellow looked at me like, "Oh, great, this old fat female has nothing else to do but come to my ER to put me through Hell." Well, as things worked out the PA came back from looking at the films and told me that I indeed had a fracture and the surgery would be the next morning. "Great, so, do you think that I might have some pain medicine now?" I was swept upstairs to bed and in traction faster than you could say "oops".

Next morning early I was carted off to the OR and met my surgeon. He was pleasant and explained the entire procedure and off he went. I didn't see him again until I was discharged. The anesthesiologist explained that he was going to give me spinal anesthesia and before I could feel the prick I was in LA-LA Land. He had given me something to put me into twilight sleep. Somewhere along the way I remember seeing bright lights and hearing BAM-BAM. I thought they were giving me an artificial hip. Then, nothing until I woke up in my bed.

Two nurses were next to me fiddling with a machine hooked to my IV. They were whispering, "Why is it doing that? Why does it say that? You know we're going to have to increase the rate if it doesn't start soon." I knew they were messing about with my morphine drip. The kind the patient gets to give their own dose when they need it. In my head I was saying, "Give it to me I'll fix it!" My pain was intense at that point and let's face it I work with these machines and could set them up in my sleep.

The morphine diminished, but did not completely help my pain. Having been on chronic morphine for over a year for my fibromyalgia I probably should have been on a higher dose. When the machine was taken away, I was given the choice of morphine IV, tramodol by mouth, or Percocet by mouth. I took Percocet. I knew the morphine would never be adequate. Six days post op and I had to decide where I wanted to go for rehabilitation. I chose my own hospital as it has a very good reputation for such. I had my kids pack some things for me and got into the ambulance for a very bumpy trip, thirty six miles down the road. As I did not work on this rehab floor, I did not tell anyone who I was or that I worked in the hospital. Patients who announce they are nurses are often pains in the ass and I did not want to be labeled. I was treated super well. Of course word leaked out and a flower came from the president's office and then at 2:00 o'clock AM some of the people I work with came down to find out what was up. The support was gratifying.

What was more gratifying was my mood had remained stable through it all. No depression due to major injury, pain, surgery, rehab and inactivity. God is good. After ten months of grievous misery with the mixed state and demoralizing depression, I was out of the woods. If I could handle all this excitement and pain, then I was better.

January 1, 2002, I went back to work at a desk job, four hours a day until I was able to run up and down the halls as usual. This would take another entire year. A year of many physical ups and downs and several mental ones too. I have many more years to come and most certainly many more highs and lows. Some will last days or weeks, some months, but here I am, 56.

END

EPILOG

I am now 62 years old. There have been a few ripples in my pond over the years, but with my doctor's and God's help-a week or two or a month or two off, the ripples disappear and I go about my business as a registered nurse in a large hospital in Baltimore, Maryland. I am considered a high functioning bipolar who understands the problems involved and am compliant with my treatment. This makes all the difference in my quality of living. I have included an index to include the life chart mentioned in this piece and the medicines I have taken over the years so it can be evident that some people take a lot of fine tuning to get things right. This so no one should become too discouraged. This list is considerable and may be helpful to those just starting their journey into the realm of their own dragons.

INDEX

MEDICATION SHEET

ALLERGY OR SENSITIVITY TO:

PT'S NAME:

SHERMAN, P.

DATE	DRUG	NO. OF PILLS	FREQ.	REFILLS (0, 1, 2)	PHYSICIAN	REASON FOR CHANGE	SEEN BY M.D.	NOT SEEN BY M.D.
1/2/88	Li₂CO₃ 300mg		πbid T↓↑					
"	Propranolol 10mg	90	↑ tid					
"	↑Propranolol 10mg	-0-	Tqid					
3/14	Propranolol 10mg	120	Tqid	Rx2		3/4 Li - 0.93		
3/28	Inderal 60mg LA	0	T qAm	-0-				
5/2	↓ LiCO₃ 300mg	-0-	πbid	-0-		maintain level		
5/23	↑Li₂CO₃ 300mg	150	πAm πhs	Rx2		Hypomanic sx↓ 2° ↓ Li level		
"	Clonazepam 0.25mg	20	πhs πAm	-0-				
6/6	Verapamil 80mg	60	πbid T↓↑ πdx2d, Tqid			3d % depressed lab. te (fearful) agitation d. sleep/appetite		
"	Cont Clonazepam, Lithium.					↓ Li level		
6/13	Verapamil 240mg SR	60		Rx2		↓ LB - 0.91		
"	Inderal 60mg LA	60		Rx1				
8/20	D/c Clonazepam							
9/9	Verapamil SR 240mg	60	T qAm	-0-				
"	Verapamil 120mg	60	πhs	-0-				
9/22	D/c all Verapamil	70	1° AV block by EKG					
10/4	Verapamil restarted @ 240mg SR qAm & 120mg qhs							
10/14	Inderal LA 60mg	60	πqAm	Rx2				
11/21	Li₂CO₃ 300mg	150	πAm πhs	Rx2		Li level 11/14 0.38 m 1500mg qd		
"	Verapamil 240mg SR	60	T qAm	Rx2				
"	Verapamil 120mg	60	T πhs	Rx2		Li level 11/20 0.74 m 1500mg qd		
12/19	↑ Li 300mg	0	πbid	0		Hypomanic ↓Li level 12/1 @↑3 (1500mg qd)		
"	Clonazepam 0.25mg	45	πAm πhs	Rx				
2/14	↓ Clonazepam 0.25mg					↓ Li Level 0.88 (1500mg qd)		
"	0.5mg	15	T qhs	Rx1				
"	Li₂CO₃ ↑ 300mg	180	πbid	Rx2				
"	↓ Clonazepam 0.5mg	0	↓ T hs x4 ⟶ D/c					
4/11	D/c Verapamil							
"	↓ Li₂CO₃ 300mg	0	πAm πhs -0-			↓ 2° tremor		

PRESS FIRMLY · BALL POINT PEN ONLY
FORM NO. 752 - 305 REV. 9/75

DO NOT USE THIS FORM
UNLESS A NUMBER SHOWS

1

PT'S NAME: SHERMAN

ALLERGY OR SENSITIVITY TO:

DATE	DRUG	NO. OF PILLS	FREQ.	REFILLS (0, 1, 2)	PHYSICIAN	REASON FOR CHANGE	SEEN BY M.D.	NOT SEEN BY M.D.
6/13/89	Verapamil 240mg SR	30	↑ hs	Rx2				
"	Verapamil 80mg	30	↑ hs	Rx2	↓ 2° near syncope			
"	Li₂CO₃ 300mg	150	↑ Am ↑ hs	Rx2	2 of will vol - 381.5 cc			
7/25/89	Li₂CO₃ 300mg	150	↑ ghs	Rx2				
7/26/89	Inderal CA 60mg	30	↑ Am	Rx2				
"	Clonazepam 0.5mg	1/0	↑ hs ↑↑	NR	Hypomania x 7 days.			
8/15	Verapamil 240mg	30	↑ hs	Rx2				
"	Verapamil 120mg	30	↑ Am	Rx2 + return.				
8/29	↓ Li 300mg	0	↑ ghs	0	c/o/s/e mild ataxia/diarrhea			
8/29	Verapamil 80mg	30	↑ Am	Rx2				
9/6	Inderal CA 60mg	60	↑ Am	NR				
9/12	Propranolol LA 60mg	60	↑ Am	NR				
10/10	Li₂CO₃ 300mg	1/0	↑ ghs	Rx✓				
10/24	Propranolol LA 60mg	60	↑ Am	✓R				
11/X	Verapamil SR 240	*30	↑ hs	Rx✓				
"	Verapamil 80mg	30	↑ Am	Rx✓				
1/2	Propranolol LA 60mg	60	↑ Am	NR				
1/16	Li₂CO₃ 300mg	120	↑ ghs	Rx2	2/2 Li - 0.99			
2/27	Li₂CO₃ 300mg	120	↑ ghs	Rx✓				
"	Propranolol LA 60mg	60	↑ Am	Rx2				
"	Verapamil 80mg	30	↑ Am	Rx2				
"	Verapamil SR 240mg	30	↑ hs	Rx2				
5/30	Verapamil SR 240mg	30	↑ hs	Rx✓	929-4404 Mann			
6/5	Tegretol 200mg	50	↑ hs x2 ↑ bid x3 ↑↑ bid x4	Rx1	↑ Δ 2° Hypothyroidism			
"	7/6 Li on taper							
"	D/c Propranolol & Li							
7/11	D/c Tegretol				severe oversedation, nausea, pallor			
"	Li₂CO₃ 300mg	0	↑ ghs	—				
"	Propranolol LA 60mg	0	↑ bid	—				

Hypothyroidism dx 4/90

MEDICATION SHEET

PT'S NAME: SHERMAN

ALLERGY OR SENSITIVITY TO:

DATE	DRUG	NO. OF PILLS	FREQ.	REFILLS (0, 1, 2)	PHYSICIAN	REASON FOR CHANGE	SEEN BY M.D.	NOT SEEN BY M.D.
1/3	Verapamil SR 240mg	30	↑ hs	Rx 2				
	Verapamil 80mg	30	↑ Am	Rx 2				
	Li₂CO₃ 300mg	120	↑ ghs	Rx 2		7/24 Li - 1.15 @ 1200mg ghs		
	↓ Li₂CO₃ 300mg	—	↑↑ ghs	—				
	Propranolol LA 60mg	60	↑ qd	R⁰¹				
8/7/90	Verapamil SR 240mg	60	↑ hs	Rx 1				
	Verapamil 80mg	60	↑ Am	Rx 1				
11/6/90	Li₂CO₃ 300mg	100	↑↑ hs	Rx 1		11/6/90 Li - 0.77 @ 900mg ghs		
	Depakote 250mg	50	↑ Am ↑↑ hs	Rx 1	2° mixed state			
	Klonopin 0.5mg	30	↑ hs prn	NR				
	D/c Verapamil on taper							
1/10	↑ Li₂CO₃ 300mg	hs	↑↑ hs	—				
1/17	Valproate 250mg	15	↑ Am ↑↑ hs					
	Depakote 250mg	100	↑ Am ↑↑ hs					
1/28	Valproate 250mg	100	↑ Am ↑↑ hs	Rx 1				
2/5/91	D/c Li on taper ↑ 300mg qod							
2/2/91	Valproate 250mg	100	↑ Am ↑↑ qd	Rx 2				
3/7/91	Valproate 250mg	100	↑ Am ↑↑ hs	Rx 2				
4/91	Prozac 20mg	30	↑ q Am	NR	Severe depression			
4/13/91	Li₂CO₃ 300	100	↑↑ hs ↑ Am	NR				
4/18/91	Prozac 20mg	100	↑ Am	NR				
4/16/91	Inderal LA 60mg	30	↑ Am	NR				
	D/c Prozac				↓ bladder S/E.			
8/9/91	Li₂CO₃ 300mg	100	↑ Am ↑↑ hs	Rx 1				
	Valproate 250mg	100	↑ Am ↑↑ hs	Rx 1				
	Inderal LA 60mg	30	↑ Am	Rx 1				
10/9/91	D/c Li₂CO₃							
	D/c Inderal							
10/9/91	Valproate 250mg	100	↑ Am ↑↑ hs	Rx 1				

PATIENT'S NAME: _SHERMAN_ INITIAL MEDICATIONS: Prednisone Ectabs } severe asthma
ALLERGY OR SENSITIVITY TO: Theodur Ceftin } non x 3 mos. ① 11/5/91
Proventil
Hypothyroidism dx 4/90   ventolin Provera / Premarin

DATE	DRUG	# OF PILLS	FREQ.	REF-FILLS	PHARMACY NUMBER	REASON FOR CHANGE
1/9/92	Valproate 250mg	100	↑Am ↑hs	Rx1		
	Klonopin 0.5mg	30	1qd prn	NR		
1/16/9~	Valproate 250 mg	100	↑Am ↑hs	Rx~		stable.
1/4/9~	↑ Depakote 500mg	100	T bid	NR		hypomania x 3wks ⓢ heartburn.
	D/C Valproate 250mg x 3day then Depakote					↗
	↑ Klonopin 0.5mg	100	½ bid ↑-↑hs NR			
1/29/9~	Valproate total dose		12.50mg qd			mixed states / depression, mania
	Li 300mg	100	Tq Am↑hs Tb.d x2 ↑Am↑hs			
1/4/9~	↓ Klonopin 0.5mg		hs	↑hs		
1/11/9~	D/c Klonopin			not needed.		
1/25/9~	D/c Li 300mg	hs	↑q3rd d			
	Valproate 500mg	120	T bid	Rx1 } total 1250mg qd		
	Valproate 250mg	100	↑qd	NR		
	D/c Inderal					Valp level 29 @ 1250mg qd.
1/8/9~	Valproate 500mg	120	T bid	Rx 2		
	↑ Valproate 250mg		T bid x 1 wk then total 1750mg qd			hypomanic
1/6/8~	Valproate 500mg	90	↑Am↑hs	Rx		
1/4/~	↓ Valproate 500mg	120	↑ bid	NR		12/93
1/9/3	Valproate 500mg	has	↑Am↑hs (as has been on the)			depression x 3wks
2/1/9~	Li CO₃ 300mg	100	↑hs ↑qhs x3 ↑qhs x3	Rx1		hypomanic x 1st month (inc. valproate)
	D/c Valproate ↑ 4 days.					
6/9~	↑ Li to 1200mg qd x2d → 1500mg qd					severe mania / insomnia
	↑ Klonopin 0.5mg	has	Max 4.0mg qd prn			
2/9~	Klonopin 0.5mg	60	2-4 mg prn	NR		calmer but sxs persist.

PATIENT'S NAME: Sherman, P.   INITIAL MEDICATIONS: Synthroid
Inhaler
ALLERGY OR SENSITIVITY TO: Trilosate
Flexeril prn

Hypothyroidism
Asthma
obesity
lumbar Pain.

DATE	DRUG	# OF PILLS	FREQ.	REF-FILLS	PHARMACY NUMBER	REASON FOR CHANGE
4/2/93	D/C Li		nausea cramp	tremor	(4/2)	Li - 1.76 @ 1500mg qd x 3d.
5/11/93	Li 300mg	hs	ghpm iii qhs x3 iii qhs			6/11 Li - 0.51 @ 900mg qd (24 hrs last dose)
1/22/93	Inderal LA 60mg	60	i bid prn	NR		
	Li₂CO₃ 300mg	100	iii qhs	Rx2		
9/12/93	Inderal LA 60mg	100	i bid prn	Rx1		2° Li tremor c benefit
1/22/93 (10/1/93)	Li₂CO₃ 300mg	100	iii qhs	Rx4		
10/1/93	Synthroid 1mg			—		by Dr Esk 2° ↑TSH c nl T₃4, T₄
3/16/94	↓Synthroid 0.075mg	—	qd			Dr D. Esk
5/12/94	Trilosate				for hip arthritis
	Li₂CO₃ 300mg	100	iii qhs	Rx5		stable
	Klonopin 0.5mg	30	qd prn	Rx1		5/24/94 0.96 @ 3³⁰pm @ 900mg qd.
	Inderal LA 60mg	hs	qd PRN		D/C'd Dr Esk 2° (may cause sympt single dose substitut) 2° asthma
10/18/94	Li₂CO₃ 300mg	100	iii q6h	NR	mailed to pt.	
12/6/94	Li₂CO₃ 300mg	100	iii qhs	Rx5		stable.
4/24/95	Li₂CO₃ 300mg	100	iii qhs	Rx5		
	Inderal LA 60mg	hs	very	irreg.		
	Klonopin 0.5mg	30	i qd prn	Rx2		
	Synthroid 0.075mg	100	qd	NR		ran out x 3-4 wks then ↓mood x 2 wks
4/27/95	Zoloft 50mg	30	½ Amqd i qd AM	NR	(410) 939-4404	depressed/labile/crying x 36 hrs
5/9/95	Zoloft 50mg	100	i qd AM	NR	"	"85% better" 7/1/95 Li - 0.77 @ 900
7/24/95	D/C Zoloft	—				pt d/c'ed 7/14/95 (½ 0.5 stability 3wk 9hr
11/6/95	Synthroid 0.075mg	100	i qd	Rx1		stable
	Li₂CO₃ 300mg	200	iii qhs	Rx6		

SUBURBAN PSYCHIATRIC ASSOCIATES

David W. Goodman, M.D.
Director
Andrew G. Feinberg, M.D.
Susan Silberman, M.D.
Valerie Goodman, M.S., L.C.S.W.-C

Johns Hopkins at Green Spring Station
10751 Falls Road
Falls Concourse, Suite 306
Lutherville, M.D. 21093
Office (410) 583-2723

MEDICATION SHEET

ALLERGY OR SENSITIVITY TO:

Synthroid — Hypothyroid
Inhaler — Asthma
motrin/ASA — obesity
ultrim — lumbar
Proveral Estrostem
Climara

DATE	DRUG	NO. OF PILLS	FREQ.	REFILLS (0, 1, 2)	PHYSICIAN	REASON FOR CHANGE	SEEN BY M.D.	NOT SEEN BY M.D.
13/96	Klonopin 0.5mg	30	t gd	Rx	939-4404			
6/96	Li₂CO₃ 300mg	120	ii qhs	Rx4		hypomania x 2 wks.		
20/96	Li₂CO₃ 300mg		iii qhs	—	Hypomania; 2° Li-1.14 ↑ nausea, diarrhea, taking.			
	Inderal 20mg	#15		on-		Li tremor		
	Zoloft 50mg	#35	↑ Am		start if tremor persist > 1wk			
2/17/96	dc Zoloft				not started.			
4/96	Li₂CO₃ 300mg	120	iii qhs	Rx4	stable. (6/97: remained on 900mg qd)			
	Klonopin 0.5mg	30	TBS	No NR				
4/97	Zoloft 50mg	#14	↑ Am	—	manic x 2 day → depressed 10 day			
	Klonopin 0.5mg		as	1/4-1/2 gd	(Pt had D/Ced) agitated.			
	dc Klonopin			only taken 3 days.				
8/97	Zoloft 50mg	100	↑ Am	NR	euthymia			
7/97	dc Zoloft	25mg qd + 2wks		+ eval GI Sx 5. (pain)				
	Li₂CO₃ 300mg	100	iii qhs	Rx5	stable.			
8/97	Klonopin 0.5mg	30	TBS	NR	272-3101			
9/98	Klonopin 0.5mg	60	TBS	NR	depressed x 1wk			
	Paxil 20mg	#35	↑ Am					
	Li₂CO₃ 300mg	100	iii qhs	Rx5				
2/98	Paxil 20mg		TBS	Rx	40-50% better			
	Paxil 40mg		TBS	—	curr. (Pt has meds.)			
10/98	Paxil 30mg	60	5mg x7, 30mg qd	Rx2	70% better @diarrhea			
	Klonopin 0.5mg	60	iii qhs	NR				
13/98	Paxil 20mg	#70	30mg Am	—	2° middle insomnia.			
	Ambien 10mg	30	TBS	NR				
13/98	dc Klonopin				euthymic			
13/98	dc Paxil 10mg	10mg qd x7 ⇒ D/c						
13/98	Li₂CO₃ 300mg	100	TBS	Rx5	410-292-3101			
	Ambien 10mg	30	TBS	NR				
1/98	Celexa 20mg	#14	TBS x qd		depressed			
11/98	Celexa 20mg	30	qam	Rx1	max ↑ to 2 qhs 2° diarrhea.			

SUBURBAN PSYCHIATRIC ASSOCIATES

David W. Goodman, M.D.
Director
Andrew G. Feinberg, M.D.
Susan Silberman, M.D.
Valerie Goodman, M.S., L.C.S.W.-C

Johns Hopkins at Green Spring Station
10751 Falls Road
Falls Concourse, Suite 306
Lutherville, M.D. 21093
Office (410) 583-2723

MEDICATION SHEET

ALLERGY OR SENSITIVITY TO:

SHERMAN, P. — provera
                Synthroid
                ultram

DATE	DRUG	NO. OF PILLS	FREQ.	REFILLS	PHYSICIAN	REASON FOR CHANGE	SEEN BY M.D.	NOT SEEN BY M.D.
10/98	Tegretol 100mg	120	Ths x3	III hs	NR	mixed stated x2wks		
	Klonopin 0.5mg	60	i-Ths	NR				
4/98	Celexa 20mg		xqhs	—		tried ~ 1wk oversedated		
	↓ Tegretol 100mg	has	Ths					
8/99	P Tegretol 100mg	100	200mg bid x1 300mg			mixed, very agitated		
	Risperdal 1mg	#30	½ Ampm Ths					
	Klonopin 0.5mg	60	iii qhs	NR				
12/99	Klonopin 0.5mg	60	iii qhs					
	Tegretol 200mg	100	iii qhs	Rx3				
	Dc Risperdal	taper	½ hs x 3d			? need.		
6/99	Klonopin 0.5mg		ths x 7 → D/c			? need.		
1/99	LiCO₃ 300mg	100	iii qhs	Rx5 272.3101				
7/99	Dc Tegretol					nausea		
	Carbatrol 300mg	#90	qhs	—				
	Celexa 20mg	30	½ qhs	Rx1				
14/99	Ambien 10mg	30	I hs prn	NR 575.7225				
12/99	Carbatrol 300mg	#90	qhs	—				
	Celexa 20mg	30	½ qhs	—				
1/99	Risperdal 1mg	has	½ bid			agitated/depressed/angry x2d.		
	Klonopin 0.5mg	has	Ths					
	Tegretol 200mg	30	½ qhs	Rx1 total 400mg qhs				
	Risperdal 1mg	30	½ bid	Rx1 410.272.3101 called in 10/11/99				
	Klonopin 0.5mg	30	i qhs					
5/99	Carbamazepine	has	500mg qd x5, 600mg qd			still mixed		
	Carbatrol 300mg	#60	above					
	LiCO₃ 300mg	100	iii qhs	Rx2				
	Carbatrol 200mg	#30	above					
9/99	Ambien 10mg	30	½ qhs iii	NR				
8/99	LiCO₃ 300	100	iii qhs	NR 272.3101				

SUBURBAN PSYCHIATRIC ASSOCIATES

David W. Goodman, M.D.
Director
Andrew G. Feinberg, M.D.
Susan Silberman, M.D.
Valerie Goodman, M.S., L.C.S.W.-C

Johns Hopkins at Green Spring Station
10751 Falls Road
Falls Concourse, Suite 306
Lutherville, M.D. 21093
Office (410) 583-2723

MEDICATION SHEET

Sherman, P.   Provera
Synthroid
Ultram

ALLERGY OR SENSITIVITY TO: _____

DATE	DRUG	NO. OF PILLS	FREQ.	REFILLS (0, 1, 2)	PHYSICIAN	REASON FOR CHANGE	SEEN BY M.D.	NOT SEEN BY M.D.
2/7/99	Celexa 20mg	30	ī ghs	Rx1				
	Carbatrol 200mg	30	ī hs	Rx3				
	Carbatrol 300mg	30	ī ghs	Rx3				
	D/C Klonopin					Stop in 3 day		
	D/C Risperdal							
10/99	Klonopin 0.5mg	30	ī qhs	Rx1	272-3101			
	Risperdal 1mg	30	ī hs	Rx1				
1/24/2000	D/C Klonopin					D/C 2° lethargy		
	Risperdal 1mg	30	ī hs	Rx2		↓ 2° lethargy		
	Tegretol 200mg		ī bm 2 ī hs	Rx2				
	D/C all carbatrol					2° expense		
1/13/00	Ambien 10mg	30	ī hs		272-3101			
	Li₂CO₃ 300mg		īīī hs	Rx2				
1/11/00	Tegretol 200mg	75	2 ī ghs	Rx3				
	Li₂CO₃ 300mg	90	īīī ghs	Rx3				
	Ambien 10mg	30	ī hs prn	NR				
7/31/00	Risperdal 1mg	60	īī qd prn	Rx1	272-3101	Not called in yet		
8/7/00	Risperdal 1mg	has	ī qd			Pt. Med		
11/8/00	Celexa 20mg	30	ī ghs	Rx1	272-3101	Depression + Today		
10/27/00	Risperdal 1mg	60	īī hs prn	Rx1	272-3101			
7/20/00	Tegretol 200mg	75	īī qd	Rx3	272-3101			
	Li₂CO₃ 300mg	90	īīī ghs	Rx3				
	Celexa 20mg	30	ī ī hs	Rx1		try in Am 2° ↓ sleep		
1/12/00	D/C risperdal							
	Tegretol 200mg	75	2 ī hs	Rx2				
	Celexa 20mg	30	ī ghs	Rx3				
1/29/00	Tegretol 200mg	has	īīī ghs	—		mixed state (hypomanic)		
	Risperdal 1mg	has	ī bid	—				
	Klonopin 0.5mg	has	ī hs	—				

SUBURBAN PSYCHIATRIC ASSOCIATES, LLC

MEDICATION SHEET

PT. NAME: SHERMAN, P

ALLERGY OR SENSITIVITY TO: _____ MEDS: Synthroid 100mcg qd 2/6/01

DX. CODE: 296.63

Date	Drug	#	Freq.	Refill	Pharmacy #	Reason for Δ
12/5/00	Neurontin 100mg #30	30	t-tid x 3d	—		mixed state
	Neurontin 300mg	100	Tbid x 4d	NR		
	Celexa 20mg	has	ī qhs	—		
	Risperdal 1mg	has	ī qhs	—		
	Klonopin 0.5mg	has	ī qhs	—		
12/12/00	Tegretol 200mg	90	īī qhs	Rx2		Hypomanic
	Klonopin 0.5mg	60	ī-īī qhs	Rx2		
	Risperdal 1mg	60	īī qhs	Rx2		
12/15/00	↑ Neurontin 300mg		īī bid			mixed state
	then D/c Celexa					may be → mixed cycling
	↑ Klonopin 0.5mg	has	īīī qhs			
	↑ Risperdal 1mg	has	īīī qhs			
	Neurontin 300mg	21 / 21	as directed (total 1200mg qd)			lace tempns.
1/3/01	Li₂CO₃ 300mg		īīī qhs	}	D/c meds from SEPH	6 day adm
	Tegretol 200mg		īī qhs			
	Neurontin 300mg		ī AM īī hs			
	Risperdal 3mg		ī hs			
	Klonopin 1mg		ī qhs			
	Wellbutrin SR150 #22		ī AM x 3 d ↑ ī bid			remains depressed not suicidal.
1/10/01	Neurontin 300mg	150	ī AM īī hs	Rx1		
	Ambien 10mg	30	½-1 hs			
	Li CO 300mg	108	īīī qhs	Rx1		
1/17/01	Wellbutrin SR 150mg	60	ī bid	Rx1		
2/5/01	D/c Ambien				A D/c x 7d ? need	
2/5/01	Risperdal 1mg curr ...	08		2/5/01 SEPH adm x 4 days	severely depressed
2/12/01	Risperdal 1mg	60	īī HS	2	410-272-3101 qd	
2/14/01	D/c Neurontin over 3 days				lethargy	

SUBURBAN PSYCHIATRIC ASSOCIATES, LLC

MEDICATION SHEET

PT. NAME: PAT SHERMAN

ALLERGY OR SENSITIVITY TO: _____

MEDS: 2/01 Synthroid 100 mcg qd.

DX. CODE: 296.53

Date	Drug	#	Freq.	Refill	Pharmacy #	Reason for Δ
2/14/01	Risperdal		hs 1 mg hs			
	D/c Klonopin					2° drowsy
2/23/01	D/c Wellbutrin					D/c when nausea diarrhea
	↑ Risperdal 1 mg. hs +hs			—		
	↓ Li₂CO₃ 300 mg		III hs	—		
	↓ Tegretol 200 mg	1	II qhs	—		↓ on 2/19 2° shakey, diarrhea nervous.
3/20/01	D/c Risperdal					
	Zyprexa 5 mg #		II hs +hs euw.			may ↑ to II hs
	Li₂CO₃ 300 mg	90	III hs Rx1			
	Tegretol 200 mg	60	II qhs Rx1			
	Zyprexa 2.5 mg		II hs euw.			
	Paxil 10 mg	#7	qd x 4d			depressed (7° relapse)
	Paxil 20 mg	#7	qd			
	Ambien 10 mg		hs hs	—		Just for DFA
3/15/01	↓ Li₂CO₃ 300 mg		hs II hs	—		Li level 1.0 @ 900 mg qd. lithotoxic
	Zyprexa 2.5 mg	#14	hs x 4d	—		3° mild hypomania (DFA)
	Paxil 10 mg	#14	qd	—		
3/2/01	D/c Zyprexa			—		D/c x 8 days
	Paxil 10 mg	30	hs Rx2			
	Ambien 10 mg	30	hs Rx1			
5/01	↑ Li to 750 mg qhs					
	Eskalith CR 450 mg	30	hs	NR		depressed
	Zyprexa 5 mg	#14	hs			
13/01	Zyprexa 5 mg	30	hs Rx1			
	D/c Ambien					not needed
7/01	Tegretol 200 mg	60	II qhs Rx2			
	Li₂CO₃ 300 mg	60	II qhs Rx2			
	Lamictal 25 mg	#45	hs x 5			depressed
	↑ Paxil 10 mg		II hs	≥ 1½ hs		

SUBURBAN PSYCHIATRIC ASSOCIATES, LLC

MEDICATION SHEET

PT. NAME: SHERMAN, PAT

ALLERGY OR SENSITIVITY TO:

MEDS: Synthroid 100mcg qd   ultram prn
2/01
9/00 MS contin 30 bg bid → Δ to morphine 9/01

DX. CODE: 296.53

Date	Drug	#	Freq.	Refill	Pharmacy #	Reason for Δ
4/17/01	d/c Zyprexa					depressed
4/1/01	Lamictal 25mg	#84	50mg qd x2wks / 100mg qd (50 bid) x2wk			much better, depressed
5/7/01	Paxil 20mg	60	Tbs x1wk, 30mg qhs NR			depressed again
5/21/01	Lamictal 100mg	#14	1 bid	—		start in 1wk.
6/13/01	Trazodone 50mg	30	Tho	NR		DFA
	d/c Ambien					
7/14/01	Lamictal 100mg	60	1 bid	Rx1	272.3101	M.S.
7/28/01	Trazodone 50mg	30	Tho	Rx1		stable x 3wks.
	Paxil 30mg	30	Tho	Rx1		
	Tegretol 200mg	120	π qhs	—		
	Li₂CO₃ 300mg	120	π qhs	—		
8/25/01	Lamictal 100mg	1mo	1 AM 1 hs	Rx.2		hypomanic x 3 days
	Tegretol 200mg	1mo	π qhs	Rx x2		
	Li₂CO₃ 300mg	1mo	π qhs	Rx2		8/01 Li - 0.5 @ 600mg
9/13/01	Paxil 30mg	30	Tqd	Rx2	575.7225 MC	Teg - 6 @ 400mg
9/10/01	Li₂CO₃ 300mg	90	π/π qhs	Rx2		mild dysthymia
	Tegretol 200mg	60	Tho	Rx2		
10/01	Lamictal 100mg	1mo	1 AM 1 hs	R+2		
11/14/01	Paxil 30mg	30	Tqd	R+2	410.272.3101	
12/01	Tegretol 200mg	180	Tho	Rx1		
	Lamictal 100mg	90d	1 AM 1 hs	Rx1		
	Paxil 30mg	90	Tqd	Rx1		
	Li₂CO₃ 300mg	90d	π/π hs	Rx1		
6/01	Ambien 10mg	30	½ Tho prn NR	272.3101 MC		
7/01	Tegretol 200mg	180	Tho	Rx1		stable
	Lamictal 100mg	90d	1 AM 1 hs	Rx + 1	returned 9/4/01	
	Paxil 30mg	90	Tqd	Rx1		
	Li₂CO₃ 300mg	90d	π/π hs	Rx1		

SUBURBAN PSYCHIATRIC ASSOCIATES, LLC

MEDICATION SHEET

PT. NAME: SHERMAN, PAT

ALLERGY OR SENSITIVITY TO: NKDA

MEDS: 2/03 Synthroid, MS Contin

DX. CODE:

Date	Drug	#	Freq.	Refill	Pharmacy #	Reason for Δ
9/8/01	R/ Paxil	hs/d	40mg qd	—		depressed.
	P Lamictal 100mg	hs/d	i Am i hs	—		
	Risperdal 1mg	hs/d	i hs	—		
9/11/01	P Li 300mg	90	II ghs	RX1		depressed
	Paxil 40mg	90	i qd	NR		
	Lamictal 100mg	270	i Am ii hs	RX1		
	Li₂CO₃ 300mg	270	II qhs	RX1		
	Risperdal 2mg	#28	i hs			anxiety/agitation.
10/4/01	P Paxil 40mg	hs/d	40mg hs x 10 / 40mg hs	—		Andrioxey.
	√ Risperdal 1mg	hs/d	½ Am	—		
	Paxil CR 25mg	# 14	(as above)	(equiv. to 10mg IR)		
11/1/01	↓ Lamictal 100mg	hs/d	i bid x 7 / i Am i hs			2° unsteady
	Paxil CR 12.5mg	#28	~ 100 hs			will taper in 2 wks.
	√ Risperdal 0.5mg	#7	i hs x 3d			? benefit Am sedation.
	Lexapro 10mg	#30	i Am	—		depressed.
	Inderal LA 80mg	60	i b.d	prn RX1		Li tremor.
10/19/01	D/C Inderal					2050 β
	P Lexapro 20mg	100	ii qhs	NR RX1		
11/20/01	D/C Paxil					off 5 days.
1/10/01	Tegretol 200mg	180	II ghs	RX1		"better"
5/10/02	Ambien 10mg	30	i QHS	NR	410-272-3101 - ok per Dr Goodman	
18/01	↓ Lamictal 100mg	hs/d	i bid	—		unsteady
2/13	Lexapro 20mg	90	i ghs	NR	410·272·3101	
4/03	P Lexapro 20mg	90d	1½ Am	NR		depressed /agitated
	Geodon 20mg	#28	i bid x 2			
	40mg	# 14	20 Am 40 hs x 7	—		
	60mg	# 14	20 Am 60 hs	—		
	Lamictal 100mg	180	i bid	RX1		
	Li₂CO₃ 300mg	270	II i hs	RX1		

Depressive Cycle 1966 to 1988

depression
mania
medication

	Jan	Feb	Mar	Apr	May	June	July	Aug	Sept	Oct	Nov	Dec	
								Mom dies	nortriptyline				1966
				Grandpa dies		Marry Byron / Pop marries Linda				Back to Finish RN Training			1967
	Graduate RN School	State Boards 1st Job 954		Pass Boards Nationals									1968
				Richard Born				Back to work / move to westminster					1969
		move to HdG											1970
								move to Lancaster / I am sole support / Byron in school / RRT					1971

Depressive Cycle 1966 to 1988

	Jan	Feb	Mar	Apr	May	June	July	Aug	Sept	Oct	Nov	Dec	
								Allan ended asthma. ulcerative colitis. Prednisone started. Big stay leave to quit school. my job in jepordy. LOA X? mo.			Emergency D+C	Spinal Headache x 2 wks	1972
						Suicidal gesture. Admit to Psychiatric LGH x 80 days	Thorazine & Psychiatric Antidpts	→			By graduates 1gwb ward	move to Aberdeen	1973
						Raped while hitchhiking	Vaginal bac infection Big bruises	← →			Byron cleaning & secretary	Start new Job C.U.H.	1974
		Depressive Antidpts				←	→				←		1975
					Grandma dies	Richard in PGH for ulcerative colitis x 35 days				Resign C.U.H.			1976
		Steel lot wakeley Goal 152			Move to H&C					Hit leew Goal, ret New Job admit for PGH. Asth, max x 15 days		PGH for duspnematic pleurory meds	1977

Depressive Cycle 1966 to 1988

	Jan	Feb	Mar	Apr	May	June	July	Aug	Sept	Oct	Nov	Dec	Year
	Start C.I.H.					Fired by FGH due to illness. Start B.A.			Federal Litigation	Resign BMH. Start HMH		Resign HMH	1978
									Antioch W. Prog. Classes. Earn B.A. Start		Find Love. Learn Irene. Byron's girl friend		1979
			Other complaint. Antipsychotic				Trial						1980
							Assault → Move to Aberdeen Apt.			Auto Accident. Car totalled			1981
	Byron beats Leticia. Replacement Antipsychotic. Admit 518 x 2wks. Very apron. discharge to Fennel			Resign CMH. Begin ANA		Divorce Trial A name	Divorce Finalized			Admit 384. BUO CAO	Begin Bypass. Surgery. Graduate from		1982
												About Job at Lawndale	1983

Depressive Cycle 1966 to 1988

Jan	Feb	Mar	Apr	May	June	July	Aug	Sept	Oct	Nov	Dec	
			Resign MCR									1984
			Resign Levindale Agency Nursing				House settlement D.N. G.P.A. [illegible] J. washington quit Agency				Return To Levindale	1985
					Pop's 2nd Cardiac cath 1 Bypass graft							1986
												1987
	Admit S.N dx Bipolar	Li_2CO_3	Pop's Cardiac Arrest $\bar{c}$ MI		verapamil			D/C verapamil due to [illegible] Heart Block	restart verapamil [illegible]		[illegible]	1988
	[illegible] $\uparrow Li_2CO_3$ due to [illegible]		D/C verapamil $\downarrow Li_2CO_3$	[illegible] restart verapamil [illegible]	$\downarrow$ verapamil due To [illegible]	Li_2CO_3 [illegible] to [illegible] dose at HS.	$\downarrow Li_2CO_3$ due To [illegible]		[illegible]	[illegible]		1989

Jan	Feb	Mar	Apr	May	June	July	Aug	Sept	Oct	Nov	Dec	
												1990
												1991
												1992
												1993
												1994
												1995

Depressive Cycle "1966 to 1988"

	Jan	Feb	Mar	Apr	May	June	July	Aug	Sept	Oct	Nov	Dec	
													1996
										Celexa Tegretol Klonopin Thorazol boy 5 milld			1997
					400 Basil Klonopin (sleep)				Lithob Celexa Tegretol respidel klonopin			1998
									Chronic Hopeless new job Good Sem		Lithob Celexa Tegretol respidel klonopin new job Good Sem	1999
				Lithob Basil Klonopin for sleep		Celexa Li₂CO₃ Tegretol					New home in Lowell Very Respidel Li₂CO₃ Tegretol klonopin respidel Neurontin allover out	Stopped /Fight X6 days Suicidal	2000
	400mg respidel Tegretol Klonopin Wellbutrin No Geodon	Lithob respidel 425 Lithob Rest Lowell Tegretol Geodon on shock therapy disability				Fight by i OH?	Terminated from OSH on first day bam bam disability Starts			en shock therapy disability	Stopped Flight X first X Suicidal	2001

	Jan	Feb	Mar	Apr	May	June	July	Aug	Sept	Oct	Nov	Dec	
2002	Back to work I am Arthritis	Why came her op cracked then	sick my by then disability	MRI will exceed B bone misplace									
2003													
2004													
2005													
2006													
200?